WITHDRAWN

CORPORATE GOVERNANCE AND ENTREPRENEURSHIP

CORPORATE GOVERNANCE AND ENTREPRENEURSHIP

Faith Ntabeni-Bhebe

www.societypublishing.com

Corporate Governance and Entrepreneurship

Faith Ntabeni-Bhebe

Society Publishing
2010 Winston Park Drive,
2nd Floor
Oakville, ON L6H 5R7
Canada
www.societypublishing.com
Tel: 001-289-291-7705
 001-905-616-2116
Fax: 001-289-291-7601
Email: orders@arclereducation.com

© **2019 Society Publishing**
ISBN: 978-1-77361-017-7 (Hardcover)

Society Publishing publishes wide variety of books and eBooks. For more information about Society Publishing and its products, visit our website at www.societypublishing.com.

ABOUT THE AUTHOR

Faith Ntabeni-Bhebe (Ph.D) specialises in research on human capital management, training and development. Performance management is one of her key areas of interest. She is the founder and managing consultant of Enhancement Consultants (www.enhancement-consultants.com).

TABLE OF CONTENTS

LIST OF FIGURES

LIST OF TABLES

PREFACE

Corporate governance in big largely listed organizations has been documented fairly extensively. This is, however, not the case with entrepreneurial small and medium-sized enterprises (SMEs) which usually include family-owned businesses. Having spent time working with clients in this sector it became clear that most view the term corporate governance and its associated guidelines as not appropriate for SMEs while others view it as an impediment that slows down their entrepreneurial pursuits. Those that have embraced it have done so only to fulfill requirements as opposed to being convinced that they can derive any value from it.

This book addresses corporate governance issues specific to SMEs with the aim of facilitating an understanding of what constitutes corporate governance in that sector. Starting with a general introduction to corporate governance and its underlying theories the book situates corporate governance in the context of entrepreneurship and entrepreneurial organizations. In doing so it decodes high-level corporate governance mechanisms ordinarily associated with big organizations to make them more applicable to SMEs.

The main pillars of corporate governance: accountability, transparency, fairness, and assurance are explored in the context of their adoption by SMEs. Guided by these main pillars the book takes the reader through how each one of these can be operationalized in an SME. The inclusion of a chapter on the interface of corporate governance and corporate social responsibility further elaborates the value that an SME can derive from good corporate citizenship. At the end of the book is a practical list of areas against which an organization can check where it stands on corporate governance issues.

This book is suitable for students, practitioners and business owners wishing to understand the value they can derive from good corporate governance. At the end of each chapter, there are sets of questions meant to check understanding and a list of reading materials to enable the reader to further engage with the issues raised.

1
CHAPTER

INTRODUCTION

Chapter Aims and Objectives

This chapter presents an introduction to Corporate Governance. By the end of the chapter you would have learned the following:

- Various definitions of corporate governance
- Key elements found in all the definitions – transparency, accountability, fairness, and independence
- Principles of corporate governance
- Main elements of corporate governance
- Evolution of corporate governance
- International organizations focusing on corporate governance
- Advantages and disadvantages of corporate governance

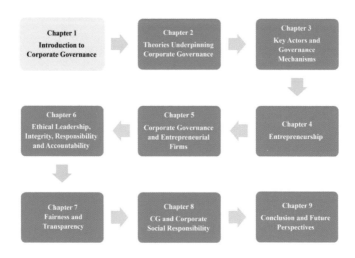

1.1. INTRODUCTION

There are various definitions of corporate governance – as many as the authorities who attempt to define it. All the definitions have the common element of balancing interests of stakeholders: owners of capital, management, employees, government and society at large. Earlier definitions emphasized one stakeholder: the owners of capital, with the Cadbury (1992) simply defining it as the system by which companies are directed and controlled. Subsequent definitions portray a more balanced perspective that includes the interest of other stakeholders (Figure 1.1).

Definitions of Corporate Governance

'... the system by which companies are directed and controlled' (Cadbury, 1992).

"... the governance of an enterprise is the sum of those activities that make up the internal regulation of the business in compliance with the obligations placed on the firm by legislation, ownership and control. It incorporates the trusteeship of assets, their management and their deployment" (Cannon, 1994).

"... the relationship between shareholders and their companies and the way in which shareholders act to encourage best practice (e.g., by voting at AGMs and by regular meetings with companies' senior management). Increasingly, this includes shareholder 'activism' which involves a campaign by a shareholder or a group of shareholders to achieve change in companies" (Corporate Governance Handbook, 1996).

"... the ways in which suppliers of finance to corporations assure themselves of getting a return on their investment" (Shleifer and Vishny, 1997).

"Corporate governance is concerned with holding the balance between economic and social goals and between individual and communal goals" (Cadbury, 2000).

'... the system by which companies are directed and controlled' (Cadbury, 1992).

"... a set of relationships between a company's management, its board, its shareholders and other stakeholders. Corporate governance also provides the structure through which the objectives of the company are set, and the means of attaining those objectives and monitoring performance are determined. Good corporate governance should provide proper incentives for the board and management to pursue objectives that are in the interests of the company and its shareholders and should facilitate effective monitoring" (OECD 2004).

Figure 1.1: Definitions of Corporate Governance.

Key elements that emerge from the definitions are that corporate governance involves:

- Exercising direction and control;
- Ensuring that shareholders get a return for their investment;
- Compliance with regulations;
- Trusteeship of assets;
- Encouragement of best practice, however, defined;
- Balancing economic and social goals;
- Balancing individual and communal goals;
- Incentivize the board and management to act in the interest of the company and its other stakeholders;
- Good corporate citizenship.

Charkham (1994) highlighted two basic principles of corporate governance as that:

1. management must have the leeway to pursue organizational

objectives without undue interference from government interference, fear of unwarranted legal action and/or fear of being dislodged;

2.   the freedom to run the business must be exercised with some measure of accountability without necessarily impeding wealth creation.

The principles illustrate that much as corporate governance is about direction and control of management it is also about creating an enabling framework for management to get on with the job of responsible wealth creation. This highlights the focus on balancing stewardship and efficiency, and motivating entrepreneurship without compromising good corporate citizenship. Figure 1.2 illustrates areas covered by corporate governance and its context.

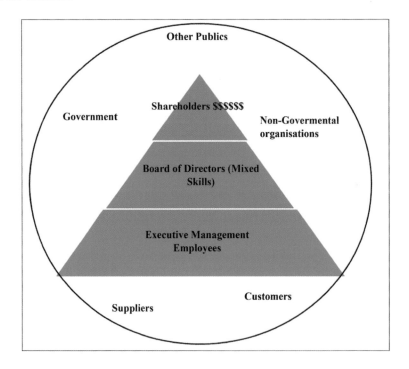

Figure 1.2: Corporate Governance Context.

1.2. HISTORY OF CORPORATE GOVERNANCE

CG is better understood from its historical perspective. Corporate governance has evolved from purely focusing on protecting the interests of shareholders to corporate social responsibility issues such as environmental concerns.

During the 1980s in the middle of the wave of mergers and take-overs in the USA and during the 1990s for Europe, corporate governance was more concerned with protecting the interests of the owners of capital. With the emergence of deregulation and integration of capital markets corporate governance also started focusing on protecting and encouraging foreign investment in emerging markets. The East Asia crises and the collapse of Bank of Commerce and Credit International during the 1990s resulted in a focus on corporate governance in emerging markets. In the UK during this period came the Cadbury report (1992), which provided a framework for corporate governance.

The early 2000s were characterized by a series of corporate scandals such as those of ENRON and World Comm which mostly concerned accounting irregularities, and the global financial crises. Focus on corporate governance was seen through the OECD adopting Principles on Corporate Governance 1999 and updating them in 2004. The UK came up with the Combined Code on corporate governance while in the US the Sarbanes-Oxley Act came into being.

Table 1.1: Evolution of Corporate Governance

Period	Impetus	Focus
1980s	Mergers and takeover wave (US)	Protecting the interests of the share-holders – the owners of capital
1990s	Mergers and takeover wave (Europe)	
	Deregulation and integration of capital markets East Asia crises Collapse of Bank of Commerce and Credit International	Protecting the interests of the share-holders – the owners of capital Protecting and encouraging foreign investment in emerging markets Corporate governance in emerging markets Cadbury report (1992) provided a framework for corporate governance – UK

2000s	Corporate scandals and failures, e.g., US ENRON and World Comm mostly concerning accounting irregularities Global financial crises	OECD adopted Principles on Corporate Governance 1999 and updated them in 2004 following a global wave of financial crises Combined code on corporate governance – UK Sarbanes-Oxley Act
2004		Combined code on corporate governance – UK
2010		UK corporate governance code (2010)

1.3. CORPORATE GOVERNANCE STYLES

Organizations have different styles of CG. The style practiced by an organization is determined partly by the relationship between the Board and Management. Addison (2006) identified four different styles:

- Chaos Management.
- Entrepreneurial Management.
- Marionette Management.
- Partnership Management.

1.3.1. Chaos Management Style

In a chaos management style of corporate governance both management and the board do not have much say in the company's strategic management process. The board is reactive as it waits for management to bring proposals to it. Management focuses on implementing the strategies of the founding entrepreneur with no strategic management being done.

1.3.2. Entrepreneurial Management Style

In entrepreneurial management there is a highly involved executive management and an uninvolved board of directors. The board exists as a rubber stamp of management decisions that are dominated by the CEO and the top management team.

1.3.3. Marionette management style

In a Marionette management style the board is involved in making the strategic decisions while management focuses on operations. In this style, the board is dominated by shareholders who are reluctant to delegate strategic issues to management.

1.3.4. Partnership Management Style

In a Partnership Management style management and the board are highly involved and work closely on the organization's strategic issues. The Board has active committees that focus on different aspects of management performance providing ongoing feedback. This is considered as the ideal form of board-management working relationship.

1.4. INTERNATIONAL ORGANIZATIONS FOCUS-ING ON CORPORATE GOVERNANCE

Corporate Governance is a global phenomenon with a number of international organizations focusing on its different aspects.

1.4.1. Organization for Economic Co-operation and Development (OECD)

Organization for Economic Co-operation and Development (OECD) adopted Principles on Corporate Governance in 1999 and updated them in 2004 (http://www.oecd.org/daf/ca/oecd-principles-corporate-governance-2004. htm) following a global wave of financial crises and again in 2015 (http://www.oecd.org/daf/ca/principles-corporate-governance.htm). The principles capture OECD's view that good corporate governance is not an end in itself but rather creates an environment where companies can access financing for long-term investment while at the same time ensuring that the shareholders and stakeholders receive fair treatment. Broadly the principles are:

Principle I: Effective corporate governance framework

Existence of a basis for an effective corporate governance framework that promotes transparent and efficient markets and is consistent with existing laws and clearly states the allocation of responsibilities among supervisory, regulatory and enforcement authorities.

Principle II: Protection of rights of shareholders

The framework should provide protection to the rights of shareholders and facilitate the exercising of those rights.

Principle III: The equitable treatment of shareholders

The framework should ensure that all shareholders, including minority and foreign shareholders, are given equitable treatment and are able to obtain redress should they perceive their rights as having been violated.

Principle IV: Stakeholders' role in corporate governance

The framework should acknowledge stakeholders' rights that are established by law or any other mutual agreements and promote the corporations' active co-operation with stakeholders for the betterment of all through for example wealth and job creation.

Principle V: Disclosure and transparency

The framework should ensure that all material issues concerning the organization and disclosed on time and accurately. Material issues include elements such as the financial position, the performance, the ownership structure and the governance issues.

Principle VI. Responsibilities of the board

The framework should provide for the board to provide strategic guidance to the organization and to effective monitor management while remaining accountable to the organization and its shareholders.

Although the OECD principles are not mandatory and not enforceable at law, they provide guidance and place an obligation on those entities not willing to adhere to them to explain themselves. What emerges from the OECD principles and definitions of corporate governance is that it is practiced through both internal and external mechanisms that are meant to mitigate the effects of the potential conflict between the interests of first the owners of capital and those of the agents (management) and also between the owners of capital and the other societal stakeholders.

1.4.2. European Union Guidelines

The European Union (EU) corporate governance framework is underpinned by the principle of "comply or explain." Its other two components are the board of directors that is expected to be effective in its supervision of management, has professional, international and gender diversity, and shareholders who hold both the board and management accountable for performance. European rules of corporate governance apply to listed companies only. The need for guidelines for unlisted companies is, however, noted as indicated in the EU green paper on corporate governance (European Union, 2011).

1.4.3. International Finance Corporation

The International Finance Corporation (IFC) (a part of the World Bank Group) among its goals is the promotion of corporate governance standards. Global Corporate Governance Forum (GCGF) is an International Finance Corporation (IFC) multi-donor trust fund that sponsors regional and local initiatives that address corporate governance weaknesses found in middle- and low-income countries.

1.5. OTHER COUNTRY/REGION-SPECIFIC GUIDELINES

1.5.1. King report (South Africa)

In South Africa the King Report on Corporate Governance identified seven primary characteristics of good governance:

- Discipline exemplified by the commitment by the organization's senior management to widely accepted standards of correct and proper behavior.
- Transparency – referring to the extent to which an outsider can meaningfully analyze the actions of the organization and its performance.
- Independence – being the extent to which conflicts of interest are managed so that the organization's best interests always prevail.
- Accountability – dealing with the rights of shareholders to receive information relating to the board and management's stewardship of the organization's assets and its performance.
- Responsibility – accepting all consequences of the organization's behavior both positive and negative and making a commitment to make amends as necessary.

- Fairness – acknowledging, respecting and balancing the interests of various stakeholders.
- Social responsibility – demonstrating a commitment to ethical standards and appreciating the social, environmental and economic impact of organizational activities on other stakeholders.

The global focus on corporate governance highlights its criticality. Corporate governance structures provide the necessary framework to assist organizations to achieve long-term success for their stakeholders. Surveys indicate that good governance is associated with:

- Protecting interest of business owners;
- Aligning the interests of owners and of management;
- Improved organizational performance;
- Ability to access external low-cost funding;
- Attracting genuine investors while penalizing rent seekers;
- Providing investors with property rights;
- Incentivizing entrepreneurs to invest;
- Business ethics.

1.6. RISKS AND DISADVANTAGES OF CORPORATE GOVERNANCE

Risks associated with corporate governance include: accounting risk, asset risk, liability risk and strategy policy risk.

- *Accounting risk*: This is the risk that the disclosure in the company's financial and related disclosures may not be complete, misinform whether by error or deliberately.
- *Asset risk*: This is the risk of company's assets being misappropriated by management.
- *Liability risk*: This is the risk that management may conclude agreements that expose the company to risk or create excessive obligations that go beyond what the company is able to handle.
- *Strategic policy risk*: This is the likelihood of management pursuing transactions that are in their own interest and not necessarily the best for the company.

A disadvantage of corporate governance mechanisms is that they come at a cost and are corruptible by managers at times working hand in hand with the board to a point where they become a "window dressing" exercise.

1.7. CORPORATE GOVERNANCE AND ENTRE-PRENEURSHIP

Corporate governance's association with bigger listed organizations with fragmented shareholders where even the board does not, in practice, represent the interests of the shareholders makes it difficult to implement in entrepreneurial organizations that are usually run by the owners. Further, in big listed corporations management wields a lot of power as a result of the separation of ownership from management with the focus being on managing the relationship between owners of capital and management. The main focus therefore hinges on the current state: establishing ways of monitoring and incentivizing management as representatives of the owners of capital to act in a manner that is in the best interest of the shareholder and in that way overcome the problems associated with separation of ownership from corporate management. This approach to corporate governance does not directly address governance issues relating to small and medium-sized enterprises (SMEs) where ownership tends to be concentrated in a few individuals or even one individual or family. In such setups ownership is not separated from management so that the problem of management being agents of the shareholder does not arise. Further, corporate governance in its regular format focuses on establishing controls on the current state an approach that can be a problem in entrepreneurial organizations as their focus is on continuously challenging the current state with a view of creating a better future state.

With SMEs and entrepreneurial companies in mind, corporate governance frameworks are not a one size fits all but rather have to be configured to suit both the internal and external peculiarities of an organization. This includes taking into consideration the organization's ownership structure, its size and its level of maturity. Regardless of the need to establish a fit, the corporate governance framework should still be robust enough so that there is clarity on:

- Roles and responsibilities;
- Limits of authority;
- Decision-making;
- Internal controls;

•   Mechanisms for controlling risk.

Ideally an organization needs to spell out its corporate governance framework to its various publics as a way of limiting misunderstandings. Figure 1.3 is an example of a Japanese company's guiding policies relating to CG.

Basic Policies on Enhancing Corporate Governance

IHI Corporation will work to enhance its corporate governance in line with the following basic policies.

1. Respect shareholders' rights and ensure equal treatment

2. Strive to cooperate appropriately with shareholders and other stakeholders

3. Fulfill our responsibility to be accountable to stakeholders and ensure transparency by appropriately and proactively disclosing information relating to the Company

4. Clarify the roles and responsibilities of the Board of Directors, the corporate auditors and the Board of Corporate Auditors to enable them to adequately fulfill their management monitoring and supervisory functions

5. Conduct constructive dialogue with shareholders who have investment policies according with the medium- to long-term interests of shareholders

Figure 1.3: IHI Corporate Governance guiding policies (*Source*: http://www.ihi.co.jp/csr/english/governance/governance01.html).

1.8. SUMMARY AND CONCLUSION

Corporate governance refers to the rules and or guidelines for managing the relationship between owners of capital, management and other stakeholders as the company seeks to achieve its multiple and at times contradictory objectives as summarized in Figure 1.4.

Although the basic values of corporate governance may be the same: transparency; accountability; responsibility; and fair treatment, in operationalizing these organizations adopt those practices that are relevant to their circumstances. Because of differences in organizations in terms for example of ownership structures, nation or region-specific environments, how corporate governance is operationalized varies without necessary departing from its underlying objectives of transparency, accountability, fairness and independence. In that regard, this book focuses on entrepreneurial organizations most of which fall under the classification of Small and Medium-sized Enterprises (SMEs).

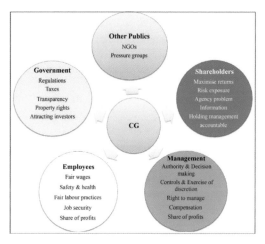

Figure 1.4: Corporate Governance Stakeholder interests.

This chapter introduced corporate governance and its various definitions. Key elements of corporate governance were identified together with OECD principles of corporate governance. The history and evolution of corporate governance together with the styles of corporate governance and key stakeholders were presented. A brief introduction to international organizations dealing with corporate governance was presented. Challenges encountered by companies in adopting corporate governance were discussed. A brief introduction to corporate governance and entrepreneurship was given. The next chapter discusses the theories underpinning corporate governance. It starts by discussing general components of corporate governance. Subsequent chapters are therefore structured as follows: Chapter 3 looks at corporate governance key actors and mechanisms. Chapter 4 discusses entrepreneurship-highlighting peculiarities of such businesses both as small to medium-sized enterprises and as family-owned. Chapter 5 discusses corporate governance in entrepreneurial firms. Chapter 6 covers ethics and integrity, responsibility and accountability. Chapter 7 focuses on fairness and transparency. Chapter 8 discusses the convergence of corporate governance and corporate social responsibility and the implications this has for entrepreneurial businesses. Chapter 9 concludes the book and provides pointers on the future of corporate governance in SMEs.

QUESTIONS AND EXERCISES

1. Discuss corporate governance stakeholder interests.

2. What role do international organizations play in advancing corporate governance?

3. That corporate governance has been widely accepted as a good practice in business does not mean that it has no limitations. Discuss giving examples.

REFERENCES AND FURTHER READING

1. Aguilera, R. V., Filatotchev, I., Gospel, H., & Jackson, G., (2008). An organizational approach to comparative corporate governance: Costs, contingencies, and complementarities. *Organization Science, 19*(3), 475–492.

2. Charkham, J. P. (1994). A larger role for institutional investors. *Capital Markets and Corporate Governance, Oxford*, 99-110.

3. European Union, (2011). The EU corporate governance framework. Brussels, 5.4.2011 COM (2011) 164 final.

4. Freeman, R. E., (1984). Strategic Management: A Stakeholder Approach, 46, Boston, MA: Pitman. Latest edition Source: The Stakeholder Paradox-Stakeholder Theory https://www.stakeholdermap.com/stakeholder-paradox.html.

5. Johnson, S., Boone, P., Breach, A., & Friedman, E., (2000). Corporate governance in the Asian financial crisis. *Journal of financial Economics, 58*(1), 141–186.

6. Keasey, K., Thompson, S., & Wright, M. (Eds.). (2005). *Corporate Governance: Accountability, Enterprise and International Comparisons*. John Wiley and Sons.

7. McCahery, J. A., & Vermeulen, E. P., (2014). Six components of corporate governance that cannot be ignored. *European Company and Financial Law Review, 11*(2), 160–95.

8. OECD, (2012). Corporate governance, value creation and growth: The bridge between finance and enterprise.

9. Pitt-Watson, D., & Dallas, G. (2016). Corporate Governance Policy in the European Union: Through an Investor's Lens. *Codes, Standards, and Position Papers, 2016*(6), 1-68.Seki, T., and Clarke, T., (2013). The evolution of corporate governance in Japan: The continuing relevance of Berle and Means. *Seattle UL Rev., 37*, 717.

10. Shadab, H. B., (2007). Innovation and corporate governance: The impact of Sarbanes-Oxley. *U. Pa. J. Bus. and Emp. L., 10*, 955.

11. Shleifer, A., & Vishny, R. W., (1997). A survey of corporate governance. *The Journal of Finance, 52*(2), 737–783.

12. Solomon, J., (2007). *Corporate Governance and Accountability*. John Wiley and Sons.

2
CHAPTER

THEORIES UNDERPINNING CORPORATE GOVERNANCE

Chapter Aims and Objectives

This chapter introduces the main theories underpinning CG. By the end of the chapter you would have learned the following:

- Agency theory
- Stakeholder theory
- Stewardship theories
- Transaction cost theory
- Resource dependence
- Social contract theory
- Political theory
- Models of CG
- Corporate Governance in Different Contexts

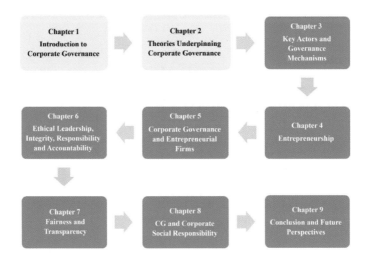

2.1. INTRODUCTION

Definitions and practices of corporate governance are guided by underlying theories which can be grouped into four guiding assumptions namely that:

- An organization is only responsible to its shareholders;
- Management cannot be trusted and needs to be controlled;
- The role of management is to maximize shareholder value;
- An organization operates within a society and is therefore responsible to that society.

2.2. AGENCY THEORY

Agency theory explains the contractual relationship between the business owner (principal, and the executive (agent). The principal is assumed to be risk neutral and is only interested in getting maximum return on the investment. The agent, on the other hand, is assumed to be self-serving only interested in those activities that do not expose him/her to unnecessary risk. Agency theory addresses this inherent conflict in the relationship (Harris and Bromiley 2007; Dalton et al., 2007). This conflict of interest is what is referred to as the agency problem and is at the root of the executive motivation problem faced by business owners. Overall agency theory as espoused by both Ross (1973), focusing on incentives, and Mitnick (2013), focusing on institutional structures, seeks to resolve problems that potentially arise when the wishes of the principal and those of the agent conflict and it is either impossible or not cost-effective for the principal to check on the work of the agent to ensure that it is in line with what was agreed. It also seeks to address problems of risk sharing that arise when the two contracting parties have differences in risk appetites which could result in the parties preferring different courses of action (Eisenhardt, 1989).

2.2.1. Criticism of Agency Theory

Although strong boards, have been said to be critical in protecting the interests of the shareholders through increasing independent director representation, empirical evidence does indicate any major improvements that can be attributed to these measures so that overall agency theory and mechanism associated with it have so far failed to address critical issues relating to executive excesses (Ozkan, 2007).

Explanations for this include that:

•   Independent directors on boards are not necessarily independent because in reality board members tend to be acquaintances of the CEO, who in fact has some influence on their appointment (Murphy, 2012).

•   The Board does not usually have sufficient information to enable them to make more informed decisions.

•   Directors on the board do not necessarily represent the interests of the shareholder so that the Board may also be more inclined to serve the personal interests of its members ignoring those of the shareholders.

•   External auditors who together with the Board are meant to safeguard the interests of the shareholders are themselves conflicted as they are appointed by management and the Board. They have been cited as among contributory factors to corporate collapse.

•   The main weakness of agency theory is its flawed assumption that independent directors on the board are independent or that they are necessarily neutral. As illustrated below cases abound of "independent" directors in fact serving the interests of the CEO. While the intention is for the board to be at the minimum objective, this is not always the case.

CG is meant to reduce agency costs in order to maximize returns, where the board is conflicted and does not act in the interest of the shareholder, agency costs have been found to escalate or to even result in collapse. Below are examples of failures of agency theory:

- Barings Bank where Nick Leeson single-handedly brought down the over 200 years old bank in 1995 (Greener, 2006);
- Enron: The Board failed to carry out its regulatory role while the external auditors were found to have knowingly assisted in the perpetuation of fraudulent activities (Petrick and Scherer, 2003);
- Bernie Madoff's 50 billion Ponzi scheme (Lenzner, 2008);
- Lehman Brothers Collapse – poor oversight by the Board in the areas of strategy and risk management (Bebchuk, Cohen, and Spamann, 2010).

2.3. STAKEHOLDER THEORY

Stakeholder theory was a response to Friedman's (1970) stockholder theory according to which an organization is only responsible to its owners. In contrast, stakeholder theory is to the effect that organizations or businesses should not only exist to achieve financial returns for its shareholders but for the benefit of all its stakeholders, both internal and external. The internal stakeholders include the obvious shareholders, management and the generality of employees. External stakeholders include governments, political parties, non-governmental organizations (NGOs), religious organizations, customers, suppliers and the general community which could be both in the immediate and the extended environment as illustrated in Figure 2.1.

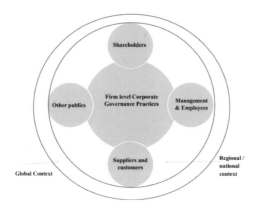

Figure 2.1: Stakeholder Theory Players.

The theory addresses the need for morals and values in the conduct of business. It adopts an open systems approach to Corp Gov and therefore considers contextual differences in its practice and recognizes the role of company-specific factors in the effectiveness of Corporate Governance. Context-specific factors refer to the interests of the various stakeholders which are bound to differ from situation to situation. An organization is viewed as behaving ethically if it attends to the interests of its stakeholders. Table 2.1 summarizes some common stakeholder interests.

Table 2.1: Stakeholder Interests

Stakeholder	Interest areas
Internal	
Shareholder	· Maximum return on capital employed · Effective management of business by executives · Kept informed of key developments in the business · Corporate governance · Executive remuneration · Risk management · Protection of rights
Management	· Substantial pay and benefits · Empowerment to make critical necessary decisions · Ability to exercise discretion · Share options · Increase in share value · Personal prestige · Boost of personal reputation
Employees	· Fair levels of pay and benefits that are paid on time · Compensation for any overtime worked · Dividend · Job security and assurance of continuity · Compliance with labor regulations · Safety and health at the workplace · Respect of rights · Opportunities for training and development
External	

Governments	· Paying taxes · Operating within stipulated rules and regulations · Environmental impact analysis · Local employment · Corruption · Standard of living · Health and safety
General public – NGOs; Pressure Groups	· Corporate social responsibility – addressing social problems · Environmental protection – pollution; biodiversity · Human rights · Regulatory compliance
Customers	· Product/service quality · Responsiveness to queries · Respecting guarantees · Responsible advertising
Suppliers	· Payment for services rendered · Fair terms of trade

Stakeholder theory has been criticized for having an unrealistic view of how and why businesses are run, not adequately addressing contradictions that may exist in stakeholder interests, and for violating the property rights of shareholders. Its focus on balancing interests has been criticized for compromising the ability of a business to operate efficiently and in the process threatening the fiduciary duty managers have to shareholders.

2.4. STEWARDSHIP THEORIES

According to stewardship theories managers are trusted stewards of the shareholder. Their motives are aligned with those of the business and to that extent their actions will always be for the corporate good. They do not need close control from the shareholder through the board as that could result in demotivation. The advantages of this approach are that it is characterized by high-levels of trust between the shareholder, board and management; hinges on principles of management empowerment; facilitates the generation of new ideas and growth. Focus is on facilitation and empowerment rather than on monitoring and controlling.

The theory is based on the assumption that every manager is well-intentioned and prioritizes the business ahead of their personal interests.

At a practical level this is rarely the case, as managers tend to engage in those activities that benefit them the most whether financially or in terms of buttressing their social standing.

2.5. TRANSACTION COST THEORY

Transaction cost theory is to the effect that the way a company is organized determines the way it controls transactions. Transaction costs refer to the level of resources, both financial and non-financial utilized in providing the products and services. When arranging business transactions managers do it in an opportunistic manner that serves their own interests without regard for monetary implications because the money is not theirs. Shareholder in this approach get residual returns – that is, whatever is left after management has fulfilled their own interests (Coase, 1937; Williamson, 1996).

According to this theory governance frameworks in organizations are guided by internal and external transaction costs that arise as the company engages in its activities. External transactions are those relating to parties outside the company while internal transactions relate to those between business units, departments and sections. Such transactions are driven by different motives on the part of directors and managers. Saravia and Chen (2008) attributed the behavior of managers to the amount of personal gain anticipated by the manager, the likelihood of being caught, and the extent to which the intended action is common practice in the company with the likely impact of these three variables on the organization determining the extent of the controls put in place.

2.6. RESOURCE DEPENDENCE THEORY

According to resources dependency theory, there is a need for linkages between the company and its environment, in that regard directors serve as a linkage between the company and its environment and through them the company gets the resources it needs to survive (Pfeiffer and Selznick, 2003). Having such linkages reduces the company's transaction costs associated with environmental uncertainties.

The theory is based on the assumption that the board is made up of people with the necessary networks to facilitate access to external resources. The performance of board members is therefore based on their contribution towards the company's attaining of competitive advantage. The assumption is that Board members bring with them key skills and value-adding networks. This is not always the case as some directors turnout to be a liability.

2.7. SOCIAL CONTRACT THEORY

Social contract theory sees society as consisting of social contracts among and between members of society and the society they live in. Companies are viewed as part of the society in which they operate and as having a contractual obligation to contribute towards the betterment of society (Donaldson and Dunfee, 1999). Related to social contract theory is legitimacy theory which is based on an assumption that a company is accountable to society in terms of how it operates because it is society that gives companies the right to utilize natural and human resources in their locale. In that regard, company performance is viewed from a triple-bottom-line approach that incorporates economic, social and environmental dimensions of performance. As the company draws from the social and environmental resources it has a responsibility to safeguard both the maintenance and replenishment of these resources and is accountable to the community.

2.8. POLITICAL THEORY

According to political theory, a country's politics affects and in itself is affected by how companies are governed (Roe, 2003). Businesses cannot be separated from the politics of their environment. Political power therefore has a say in governance matters of an organization to an extent that the allocation of power, profits and privileges within the organization depends on government's goodwill through for example direct participation in the running of companies or promulgation of laws and policies that affect the management of companies.

At a micro level the political model refers to a situation where corporate policy is changed through the actions of active investors who mobilize scattered minority investors into a meaningful block strong enough to offset purchasing voting power. According to Pound (1992) this type of governance will be more powerful but cost-effective than that derived from purchasing voting power.

2.9. LIFECYCLE THEORY OF THE FIRM

According to lifecycle theory of the firm, corporate governance evolves as a company goes through the various stages of its lifecycle. Because the rate of pay managers receive tends to be linked to the growth of the company, in order to maximize their own earnings both monetary and non-monetary, they may pursue a fast growth strategy that may not necessarily maximize shareholder value (Muller 2003). According to Toms (2013) because the resource base of a company changes as it goes through its lifecycle, its corporate governance mechanisms also change. O'Connor and Byrne (2015) found that the more mature a company was the better its overall corporate governance practices and that when companies are still young they tend to be more transparent and accountable.

2.10. CONTINGENCY THEORY

Corporate governance framework is not a one size fits all as what is adopted in an organization is a result of factors specific to that organization (Huse, 2015). Some of the organization-specific factors are:

- Geographical, national and cultural;
- Industry sector;
- Type of ownership and extent to which ownership is concentrated or dispersed;
- Size of company and the stage it is at in its lifecycle;
- Level of integration, whether part of a bigger group or stand alone;
- Type of Chief Executive Officer, their background and management and leadership style.

Based on this theory corporate governance practices in SMEs therefore differ considerably from those found in big corporates although the overall objective remains the same namely: accountability, assurance, fairness, and transparency.

2.10.1. Summary of Theoretical Approaches to Corporate Governance

The various theories of corporate governance are not necessarily mutually exclusive as they tend to overlap. Table 2.2 presents a summary of the theories and their main characteristics.

Table 2.2: Theoretical Approaches to Corporate Governance

Underlying theories	Perspective and Main components
Agency theory	Managers as agents of shareholders can engage in self-serving behavior that may be detrimental to shareholders' wealth maximization
Transaction cost theory	Managers arrange business transactions in an opportunistic self-serving manner, shareholders get residual returns.
Stakeholder theory	Stakeholders hold a stake in companies. They are affected by company activities but they in turn affect the companies
Resource dependence theory	Directors serve as a linkage between the company and its environment
Stewardship	Managers are trusted stewards of the shareholder. Their motives are aligned with those of the business. The interests of the company are paramount.
Social contract theory	Society consists of social contracts among and between members of society companies are part of the society
Political theory	A country's politics affects and in itself is affected by how companies are governed Businesses are affected by and are themselves part of the political environment
Lifecycle Theory of the firm	Corporate governance evolves as a company goes through the various stages of its lifecycle
Contingency theory	A company's corporate governance framework is determined by factors specific to the company

2.11. DIFFERENT MODELS OF CORPORATE GOVERNANCE

Clarke (2016) classifies models of corporate governance into four: Anglo-Saxon, Germanic, Latin and Japanese. Because of close similarities between the Latin and Japanese approached in this text these have been combined. Differences in approaches are based on the nature of capitalism being practiced in their environment.

2.11.1. Anglo-Saxon Approach

Anglo-Saxon countries (USA; UK; Canada; Australia and New Zealand) use the liberal model that gives priority to shareholder interests. It encourages radical innovation and cost competition. Objective is to maximize shareholder value. The shareholders are the main stakeholders that influence managerial decision-making. Directors are classified as either non-executive or executive. The economic relationships have a short-term orientation with a focus on paying for performance. The advantages of this approach to corporate governance include orientation towards dynamic markets, international orientation and therefore ability to handle fluid capital. Weakness of this approach has been identified as its short-termism which has been associated with management focusing on shirt term goals which in some cases are detrimental to a company's long-term value creation.

2.11.2. Latin and Japan

Latin (France, Italy, Belgium, Spain) and South American (Argentina and Brazil) and Japan use the coordinated model which follows a network orientation and includes workers, managers, customers and suppliers, and the community. Management decision-making is influenced by financial institutions, government, families and employees. It encourages incremental innovation and quality based competition. To a low to moderate extent remuneration is based on performance and economic relationships have a long-term approach. The strength of the approach is in its long-term strategic approach, stable capital and creating an environment of continuity in skills development, creativity, a focus on aesthetics and flexibility. The weaknesses of this approach include non-transparent governance, secretive procedures and control vested in the majority. This approach is dominated by family-owned businesses – which present a different corporate governance scenario from the liberal model and the coordinated model.

2.11.3. Germanic Approach

Germanic approach (German, Netherlands, Switzerland, Sweden, Austria, Denmark, Norway and Finland) is market-oriented represented by a mixture of networks of shareholders, families and banks. Influence on management decisions is exerted by the banks and by oligarchic groups including employees. There is generally a low relationship between remuneration and performance. The strength of the approach is in its robust governance, stable capital and long-term strategic focus. Its disadvantage is weak internalization, inflexibility, and insufficient investment for new industries.

2.11.4. Islamic Approach

Corporate governance model in Islam world has features that set it apart from forms of governance found in the Anglo-Saxon and the European models. The Islamic model is grounded in Shari'ah. While having a focus on protecting the interest and rights of all stakeholders, this is subject to Shari'ah rules. This is illustrated in the Islamic perception of ethics as dealing with ways of avoiding wrong doing and only doing what is right and desirable and one's relationship with Allah, other people, other creatures, the universe and one's innermost self. A person's conduct is judged as ethical or otherwise based on their intentions so that conduct must be done with good motives and in a manner consistent with the norms of *Shari'ah* which is the command of God revealed to the Prophet (Reinhart, 2005). The profit motive although acknowledged is balanced with Shari'ah principles and the need for distributive justice. Managers operate as vicegerents of Allah. Islam is therefore the ultimate stakeholder. In that regard, in the corporate governance system the *Shari'ah* is the governing law of everything a company does. Governance is therefore operationalized through two-tier Boards: with the ultimate governance resting with the Shari'ah board.

2.11.5. Chinese Approach

The Chinese corporate sector is dominated by state enterprises, concentrated shareholding and weak minority shareholders. Since 2001 China has corporate governance guidelines for listed companies which are captured in "Code for Corporate Governance of Listed Companies." This was followed by the 2004 "Code for Corporate Governance of Securities Companies." Both focus on the governance structures of listed companies. Notwithstanding improvements over the years generally transparency and accountability still remain weak (Feirnerman, 2007).

2.11.6. Insider-Outsider Model

In an insider-dominated system, the agency problem is reduced as a result of close ties between ownership and management so that it is easier to align the interests of the shareholders and those of management as they tend to be the same people. However, because of low levels of management-ownership separation, other problems such as abuse of power, ignoring interests of minority shareholders, limited transparency, and abuse of company assets may arise. In East Asia, the severity of the 1997 financial crisis has been partly attributed to high-levels of ownership concentration.

2.11.7. Which Model for Entrepreneurial Businesses?

Which model is more in tune with entrepreneurial businesses? Clarke (2016 40) concluded that "Essentially it seems that the different corporate governance systems may be better at doing different things, and with different outcomes for the economy and society."

2.12. SUMMARY AND CONCLUSION

The form of corporate governance adopted in any situation is derived from underlying theories the main theory being agency theory. Other theories are stakeholder, stewardship, transaction, resource dependence, social contract and political theory. Further, different countries and or regions adopt different forms of corporate governance practices. USA; UK; Canada; Australia and New Zealand are inclined towards the liberal model that gives priority to shareholder interests; France, Italy, Belgium, Spain, Argentina and Brazil together with Japan base their practices on a coordinated model which leans towards a network orientation; German, Netherlands, Switzerland, Sweden, Austria, Denmark, Norway and Finland use a market-oriented approach that has a mixture of networks of shareholders.

As a prelude to discussing corporate governance in SMEs and or entrepreneurial companies the next chapter discusses corporate governance variables. This will facilitate an understanding of the nexus of corporate governance and entrepreneurship and corporate governance and SMEs.

QUESTIONS AND EXERCISES

1. How relevant are Agency Theory and Stakeholder Theory in understanding corporate governance mechanisms?

2. Which model of corporate governance do you think is suitable for entrepreneurial companies?

3. Using an organization you are familiar with discuss the applicability of Social Contract theory to understanding corporate governance.

4. Corporate governance is the product of an organization's past. To that extent it evolves "a manner that takes tradition as a modifiable

given, not as a convention that could readily be discarded" (Yu, 2007). Discuss this statement with reference to the evolution of corporate governance in any Asian country.

REFERENCES AND FURTHER READING

1. Bebchuk, L. A., Cohen, A., & Spamann, H., (2010). The wages of failure: Executive compensation at Bear Stearns and Lehman 2000–2008. *Yale J. on Reg.*, *27*, 257.

2. Clarke, T. (2004). Theories of corporate governance. *The Philosophical Foundations of Corporate Governance, Oxon.*.

3. Dalton, D. R., Hitt, M. A., Certo, S. T., & Dalton, C. M., (2007). The Fundamental Agency Problem and Its Mitigation: Independence, Equity, and the Market for Corporate Control. *The Academy of Management Annals*, *1*(1), 1–64.

4. Eisenhardt, K. M., (1989). Agency theory: An assessment and review. *Academy of Management Review*, *14*(1), 57–74.

5. Feinerman, J. V., (2007). New hope for corporate governance in China?. *The China Quarterly*, *191*, 590–612.

6. Filatotchev, I., & Wright, M., (2005). *The Lifecycle of Corporate Governance*. Edward Elgar Publishing.

7. Filatotchev, I., Toms, S., & Wright, M., (2006). The firm's strategic dynamics and corporate governance lifecycle. *International Journal of Managerial Finance*, *2*(4), 256–279.

8. Freeman, R. E., (1999). Divergent stakeholder theory. *Academy of management review*, *24*(2), 233–236.

9. Greener, I., (2006). Nick Leeson and the collapse of Barings Bank: socio-technical networks and the 'rogue trader'. *Organization*, *13*(3), 421–441.

10. Harris, J., & Bromiley, P., (2007). Incentives to cheat: The influence of executive compensation and firm performance on financial misrepresentation. *Organization Science*, *18*(3), 350–367.

11. Huse, M., (2005). Corporate governance: Understanding important contingencies. *Corporate Ownership and Control*, *2*(4), 41–50.

12. Lenzner, R., (2008). Bernie Madoff's $50 billion Ponzi scheme. *Forbes*. Retrieved from https://www.forbes.com/2008/12/12/madoff-ponzi-hedge-pf-ii-in_rl_1212croesus_inl.html#5d730ee650b7

13. Lewis, M. K., (2005). Islamic corporate governance. *Review of Islamic Economics*, *9*(1), 5.

14. Mitnick, B. M., (2013). Origin of the Theory of Agency: An Account by One of the Theory's Originators. Retrieved from http://dx.doi.

org/10.2139/ssrn.1020378

15. Mueller, D. C., (2003). *The Corporation: Investment, Mergers, and Growth.* Routledge Taylor & Fancis Group.

16. Murphy, K. J. (2013). Executive Compensation: Where We Are, and How We Got There. *Handbook of the Economics of Finance, 2,* 211-356.

17. O'Connor, T. & Byrne, J., (2015). Governance and the corporate lifecycle. *International Journal of Managerial Finance, 11*(1), 23–43.

18. Ozkan, N., (2007). Do corporate governance mechanisms influence CEO compensation? An empirical investigation of UK companies. *Journal of Multinational Financial Management, 17*(5), 349–364.

19. Petrick, J. A., & Scherer, R. F., (2003). The Enron scandal and the neglect of management integrity capacity. *American Journal of Business, 18*(1), 37–50.

20. Pfeffer, J., & Salancik, G. R., (2003). *The External Control of Organizations: A Resource Dependence Perspective.* Stanford University Press.

21. Pound, J. (1993). The rise of the political model of corporate governance and corporate control. *NYUL Rev., 68,* 1003.

22. Reinhart, A. K., (2005). Origins of Islamic Ethics: Foundations and Constructions. *The Blackwell Companion to Religious Ethics,* 246–252.

23. Ross, S. A., (1973). The economic theory of agency: The principal's problem. *The American Economic Review, 63*(2), 134–139.

24. Saravia, J. & Chen, J. J., (2008). The Theory of Corporate Governance: A Transaction Cost Economics–Firm Lifecycle Approach. Retrieved from   http://epubs.surrey.ac.uk/id/eprint/816784

25. Toms, S., (2013). The Lifecycle of Corporate Governance. *The Oxford Handbook of Corporate Governance,* p. 349.

26. Williamson, O. E., (1979). Transaction-cost economics: the governance of contractual relations. *The Journal of Law and Economics, 22*(2), 233–261.

27. Yu, C. M. J., (2007). Networked firms in the Republic of China: Toward a hybrid shareholder model. *Best Practices in Asian Corporate Governance.* Retrieved from https://www.researchgate.net/profile/Toru_Yoshikawa2/publication/241823161

3
CHAPTER

CORPORATE GOVERNANCE– KEY ACTORS AND GOVERN- ANCE MECHANISMS

Chapter Aims and Objectives

This chapter discusses the corporate governance of key players and governance mechanisms. By the end of the chapter you would have learned the following:

- Key corporate governance actors specifically
- Shareholders
- Board
- Management
- Other stakeholders
- Internal and external governance mechanisms

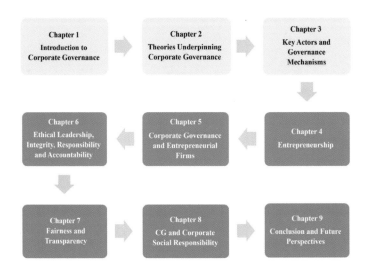

3.1. INTRODUCTION

This chapter discusses key actors in corporate governance and the specific roles they play. The actors are identified as: the shareholders both major and minor, the Board of Directors, management and other stakeholders. This chapter focuses on each one of these. The actors interact and carry out their duties using both internal and external corporate governance mechanisms. Different forms of Boards of Directors are discussed together with their effectiveness or otherwise. Internal and external mechanisms of corporate governance are highlighted specifically: strengthening of shareholders' rights; company structure; company strategy; board management monitoring; executive compensation; compliance with internal controls and independent risk and internal audit.

3.2. KEY ACTORS–SHAREHOLDERS

Shareholders are the owners of the business. They are responsible for providing the business with capital. They stand to benefit most from the success of the business and also stand to lose the most should the business fail. Shareholders come in different forms: preferred stock shareholders, common stock shareholders, institutional investors and individual investors. Preferred stock shareholders do not vote on the company's matters but receive a steady dividend that is paid ahead of common stock shareholders. In the vent of bankruptcy, they are also paid ahead of common stock shareholders. Common stock shareholders elect directors to the board, vote on company matters, are entitled to a dividend and to payment in the event of a bankruptcy though after the preferred stock shareholders. Institutional investors represent big organizations and buy large volumes of shares to an extent of affecting the share price. They usually constitute majority shareholding. Individual investors trade in smaller volumes and usually constitute minority shareholding. Shareholders are the residual claimants of a company's proceeds at they are paid last after everyone else involved in the operations of the business has been paid, hence the need for their interests to be protected. Majority and or shareholders with many shares also-called controlling blockholders, have the power to influence a company's governance systems in terms for example of the board of directors, chief executive and senior management. Such shareholders can dominate and silence minority shareholders presenting yet another governance problem. Non-institutional blockholders such as those representing families have been associated with both good and bad practices. Block holders representing institutions such as pension funds have been associated with being ineffective.

Main forms of business ownership are: public with widely dispersed shareholders, state, family, cross-held groups, partnerships and sole players. Each has different business objectives and therefore presents both general and specific corporate governance challenges.

3.2.1. Public Ownership

Most corporate governance literature focuses on publicly owned businesses or corporations. Publicly owned businesses have many shareholders who may change on a regular basis as their shares are publicly traded. Shareholders in public entities have rights that are detailed in the company's charter and its by-laws. Generally these include:

- Access to the company's books of accounts;
- Holding the Board of Directors and management to account and using them for any misdeeds;
- Receiving a proportionate share of the proceeds should the company go into liquidation;
- Receiving a share of the dividends;
- Voting on the company's issues such as major decision, for example, mergers and acquisitions who should sit on the Board of Directors
- This form of business ownership is the most regulated and faces

the most agency problems as there is a clear separation between ownership and management.

3.2 2. Private Limited Companies

Private limited companies are less regulated than the public listed businesses. These have fewer shareholders as a result there is more concentrated shareholding and therefore less risk exposure. Many family-owned businesses falls into this bracket. Given that corporate governance is more than shareholder rights it is equally critical to focus on their corporate governance issues.

CG issues faced by this type of company relate to: ownership and control, professional management role, transparency and accountability, levels of education and awareness of developments outside the company. Corporate governance becomes necessary for purposes of attracting low-cost capital, succession planning and conflict resolution. Institute of Directors (UK) summarized the concern of corporate governance in unlisted companies as that of "establishing a framework of company processes and attitudes that add value to the business and help ensure its long-term continuity and success."

The main corporate governance challenges faced by private limited companies as:

- Enhancing risk management oversight;
- Ability to assess innovation;
- Ability to assess competition;
- Ability to formulate the company's strategy;
- Regulatory and global compliance.

The challenges are compounded by that most private limited companies do not have the financial capacity to access high caliber board members as tends to be found in public companies. Where financial capacity is there, there are high-levels of conflict of interest because of the involvement of ownership in management to an extent that some may be reluctant to have outsiders looking into their operations. For example, in most such businesses there tends to be the common issue of owner-initiated related party transactions that are not always transparent.

3.2.3. Partnerships

A partnership has two or more business owner-managers. Ownership rights and responsibilities are captured in the partnership agreement. Governance risk is shared among the partners based on what is detailed in the partnership agreement. Despite this, these also tend to have corporate governance challenges similar to those in private limited companies.

3.2.4. Sole Proprietorship

A sole proprietorship is a business that is owned and run by one person. It therefore has no separation of ownership and management. All risks associated with governance are carried by the owner. This form of business has a weak governance structure as there is no separation between the business and the owner. Financial record keeping is generally poor and in some instances does not exist. With nobody playing an oversight role compliance with regulations is also generally low as it is entirely dependent on the owner.

Table 3.1: Corporate Governance Issues Specific to Forms of Ownership

Type	Characteristics	Governance Issues
Public companies	- Many shareholders - Liability of shareholders is limited - Almost unlimited ability to raise capital - Ownership can be transferred easily - No need for owner business expertize	- Many legal requirements to be adhered to including separation between management and ownership - Mandated transparency and disclosure
Private Limited	- Fewer shareholders - Liability of shareholders is limited - Does not have to answer to shareholders - Limited ability to raise capital - Transfer ownership not easy - Need some owner business expertize	- Fewer legal requirements - No requirement for independent board - Succession planning - Risk reporting and analysis - Financial transparency - Strategic planning

Partnerships	- More than one - Liability is unlimited but is shared among partners as per the partnership agreement - Limited ability to raise capital - Ownership is not transferable - Expertize in the business is required	- Fewer legal requirements - Succession planning - Risk reporting and analysis - Financial transparency - Strategic planning
Sole proprietorship	-Business owned by one person – no separation between owner and the business - Easy to form – limited legal requirements - Liability is unlimited -Ability to raise capital is very limited -Ownership transfer is only by selling the whole business - Owner expertize in the business is required	-Development and documentation of general guiding procedures and systems - Formalization of strategic planning - Development of business continuity systems - Mechanisms for managing risk

Different forms of business ownership produce different corporate governance frameworks and practices. To that extent there is no one size fits all model of CG. Subsequent chapters of this book focus on corporate governance in entrepreneurial organizations. Because of the overlap between being entrepreneurial and falling within the SME bracket, the terms may be interchanged. However, not every SME is necessarily entrepreneurial. Similarly being a large organization and being entrepreneurial are not mutually exclusive. Organizations, however, tend to transition from being entrepreneurial during the early stages of growth to being less entrepreneurial when they become established and big. Further, SMEs tend NOT to be public corporations and therefore not to necessarily have a Board of Directors where there is one it tends to operate differently from what is found in public companies.

3.3. KEY ACTORS – THE BOARD

A Board of Directors consists of individuals who are elected or selected to represent the interests of the shareholders – who are the owners of the company. The Board establishes policies to guide the management of the business and is responsible for making major strategic decisions. All public listed companies have a Board of Directors. The situation is different with private companies where there is no legal requirement to have a Board. However, in some jurisdictions private companies of a certain size are required to have a Board of Directors.

There are two types of directors: executive (inside) and non-executive (external). An 'inside' director is also referred to as 'non-independent.' Such a director is involved in the day-to-day operations of the company. For example, a Chief Executive Officer and or Finance Director are an executive director. An 'external' director is also referred to as an independent director if they do not hold any position within the company and do not hold any shareholding in the company. It is possible to have external non-independent directors. Such directors may be representing specific shareholders' interests. While such a director qualifies to be described as external, they are not necessarily independent.

When there is a high proportion of inside directors compared to external ones the Board tends to make decisions that are in favor of management represented by the inside directors. When external directors are too many compared to internal ones, decisions taken may be divorced from the reality on the ground which may have negative results on the business. The aim is to achieve a balance that serves the interests of the business and the shareholders and creates an environment that is conducive for making critical decisions and ensures that directors are able to make objective independent judgment on the affairs of the company.

3.3.1. Board Composition

While it is generally suggested that from custom and practice the ideal size of Board of Directors is seven to nine members, the size of a board is guided by the needs of the business in terms of its size, where it is in its growth cycle, the complexity of its operations and its critical stakeholders. The ideal board size is therefore that which facilitates execution of duties. When it has too many members there could be problems which include the costs of sustaining such a Board. When they are too few that could also be a problem as there could be a deficiency of some required skills as the board must have sufficient relevant skills. For example, skills such as finance, marketing, human resources management, relevant technical skills such as engineering and specific industry experience are critical. A mixture of demographic groups to reflect the society in which the business is operating is also critical.

The functioning of the Board is guided by a Board Code of conduct which addresses issues such as:

- Basic standards of conduct;
- Responsibility to the company;
- Conflicts of interest, disclosures and outside appointments;
- Confidentiality and inside information;
- Ethics, acceptance of gift or any other rewards and advantages;
- Privileges and immunities;
- Communicating with outsiders and cooperation with investigating bodies;
- Evaluation of board performance.

Figure 3.2 presents an example of a corporate governance system.

Corporate Governance System

(1) Board of Directors

The Board of Directors, which consists of 13 directors (3 from outside), makes decisions related to all important matters concerning the management of the IHI Corporation and the Group, in addition to supervising directors in their business execution.

(2) Board of Corporate Auditors

IHI Corporation has a Board of Corporate Auditors which comprises 5 corporate auditors (3 from outside) who audit the duties executed by directors.

(3) Business execution framework

IHI Corporation has an executive officer system to facilitate and strengthen the decision-making and supervisory functions of the Board of Directors, as well as to improve the efficiency of business operations. Appointed by resolution of the Board of Directors, there are 25 executive officers, 5 of whom concurrently serve as directors.

(4) Compensation Advisory Committee

To ensure that directors and corporate auditors are remunerated appropriately, IHI Corporation established the Compensation Advisory Committee as a voluntary committee, consisting of 6 members: 3 outside directors, 1 outside corporate auditors, a director responsible for human resources, and a director responsible for finance and accounting. The chair of the Committee is an outside director.

(5) Nomination Advisory Committee

Additionally, IHI Corporation established a Nomination Advisory Committee, to supervise the nomination of candidates for directors and corporate auditors by the representative director, checking that such appointments are conducted appropriately, and to offer related advice, among other purposes. The Committee consists of 5 members: the President and Representative Director, the Chief Executive Officer and 3 outside directors. , and the President and Representative Director serves as chair.

Figure 3.1: Example of a Corporate Governance System. *Source*: http://www. ihi.co.jp/csr/english/governance/governance01.html#governance01_02.

The Board of Directors is responsible for appointing the CEO, providing strategic guidance and approval, monitoring management including putting in place governance structures for the company, approving mergers and acquisitions, appointing auditors, reviewing and approving audit and financial contracts, configuring executive compensation, disciplining poorly performing executives.

The Board is also responsible for overseeing operational systems to ensure that there is compliance with relevant laws such as those relating to taxation, competition, labor, environmental, equal opportunity, and health and safety. It is its responsibility to ensure that management provides it with adequate information to facilitate appropriate decision-making.

On a regular basis the performance of the board is evaluated either by the Board itself or through third parties. Board evaluation improves board operations through facilitating better interaction between directors, identifying the strengths and weaknesses of the boards and flagging areas in which directors may need training or exposure. Figures 3.3 is an example of clearly articulated board responsibilities that make it possible to carry out an evaluation of the board's performance.

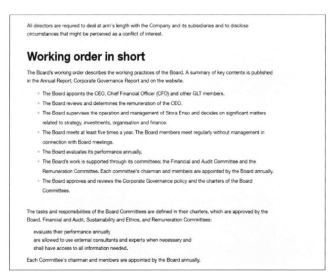

Figure 3.2: Example of clearly articulated board responsibilities. Source: http://www.storaenso.com/investors/governance/board-of-directors/composition-responsibilities-and-duties-of-the-board-.

Best practice in board functioning has been associated with the following Board attributes:

- A directors nomination and election process that ensures independence and an appropriate mix of skills;
- Maintenance of independence at both Board and Board Committees level;
- An independent Chairman of the Board;
- An accountable Board;
- Responsiveness to Shareholders;
- Regular Board renewal through election of new members;
- Timed self-evaluation of Board performance;
- Holding separate meetings of independent Board directors; separate from those that include management;
- Sourcing specialist skills such as external audit and risk assessment as necessary;
- Demanding disclosure of related party transactions.

Although at a theoretical level the role of the Board of Directors is clear: to provide strategic direction, monitor management in order to minimize agency costs while maximizing shareholder returns, reality is different. Board of Directors comes in different forms in terms of executing their responsibilities. Table 3.2 summarizes board styles and their approach to executing their duties.

Table 3.2: Board Types

Type	Practices
Old boys/girls club	Interrelated. Covering for each other. May pursue own interests. Blamed for the American corporate scandals of the early 2000s.
Rubber stamp	Management makes all the decisions with the board approving all without any further consideration.
Country club	Reviews selected issues.
Trophy	Minimum level of Board involvement, if at all.
Yes-men	Agrees with everything management does, in fact told by management what to do.
Phantom	No involvement at all – only exists by name.

Real thing	Plays a leading role in strategic planning and monitoring of implementation; has vibrant committees to focus on key business aspects and keep the Board informed.

3.4. KEY ACTORS – MANAGEMENT

The role of management as represented by the Chief Executive Officer, is to implement board directives ensuring that the company operates efficiently, implements the strategy as agreed, prepares and submits financial and other reports as per agreed standards and as required by legal, regulatory and other accepted standards. Other management responsibilities include:

- Development of operational plans consistent with approved strategic plan
- Developing risk management policies to be approved by the board of directors;
- Implementation of approved policies;
- Instituting internal controls and establishing procedures to ensure compliance;
- Implementing management information systems that are consistent with the company's assessed risk profile;
- Establishing satisfactory transparent reporting systems. This includes putting in place an organizational reporting structure that facilitates the assignment of responsibilities for risk-taking and risk monitoring, and ensures checks and balances.
- Devising mechanisms for timely addressing of deviations identified by for example internal auditors;
- Compliance with the law and other regulatory conditions;
- Establishing an effective human resources management system that supports business objectives.

Examples of management role are given in Figure 3.3.

Figure 3.3: Examples of Management role.

Kingfisher (http://www.kingfisher.com/index.asp?pageid=272) stipulates the responsibilities of its CEO in five broad areas stated as: Key responsibilities; Meetings; Directors and senior management; Relations with shareholders and other responsibilities (see Figure 3.). The responsibilities clarify the role of the CEO in running the company, interfacing with the chairman of the board and other board members, interfacing with the company's various stakeholders, accurate reporting and operating with integrity and adhering to high standards of corporate governance. While the board plays an oversight role, it is clearly the CEO's responsibility to operationalize high-levels of corporate governance in the organization.

The Chief Executive Officer reports to the Chairman (acting on behalf of the Board) and to the Board directly. The Chief Executive Officer is responsible for all executive management matters affecting the Group. All members of executive management report, either directly or indirectly, to the Chief Executive Officer.

The Chief Executive Officer is responsible for:

1. Key responsibilities

Leading the executive management of the Group's business, consistent with the strategy and commercial objectives agreed by the Board.

Leading the executive team in effecting the Board's, and where applicable its Committees', decisions.

Ensuring that the Chairman is alerted to forthcoming complex, contentious or sensitive issues affecting the Group of which they might otherwise not be aware.

Working with the Operating Companies, for researching, proposing and developing the Group's strategy and overall commercial objectives, in consultation with the Chairman and the Board.

In delivering the Group's strategic and commercial objectives the Chief Executive Officer is responsible for the maintenance and protection of the reputation of the Company and its subsidiaries.

2. Meetings

Providing input into the Board's agenda from themselves and other members of the executive team.

Maintaining a dialogue with the Chairman on the important and strategic issues facing the Group, and proposing Board agendas to the Chairman which reflect these.

Ensuring that the executive team gives appropriate priority to Board reporting in an accurate, timely and clear nature.

3. Directors and senior management

Commenting on induction programmes for new directors and ensuring that appropriate management time is made available for the process.

Ensuring that the development needs of the executive directors and other senior management reporting to them are identified and endeavoured to be met.

Providing information and advice on succession planning, to the Chairman, the Nomination Committee, and (as applicable) members of the Board.

Ensuring that Management Development Reviews regarding their executive and management duties are carried out at least annually in respect of all the executive directors. Providing input to the wider Board evaluation process.

4. Relations with shareholders

Leading the communication programme with the Company's shareholders.

5. Other responsibilities

Setting and leading the vision and purpose of the organisation.

Promoting, and conducting the affairs of the Group with, the highest standards of integrity, probity and corporate governance.

Ensuring, in consultation with the Chairman and the Company Secretary as appropriate, that the executive team comply with the Board's approved procedures, including Matters Reserved to the Board for its decision and each Committee's Terms of Reference.

Providing input to the Chairman and Company Secretary on appropriate changes to the Matters Reserved to the Board and Committee Terms of Reference.

Figure 3.4: Responsibilities of Kingfisher's CEO.

Management as agent of the shareholder, in turn is, theoretically, compensated in a manner that reflects their level of contribution and that motivates them to act in the interest of the shareholders while balancing the interests of other stakeholders.

3.5. KEY ACTORS-OTHER STAKEHOLDERS

Other corporate governance stakeholders are the rest of the employees, Non-governmental organizations (NGO), customers, suppliers, financial markets, and the community at large.

3.5.1. Employees

According to OECD employees are among the stakeholders that play an important role in the long-term success of a company. Good relations between employees and management facilitate good performance and realization of shareholder objectives. Employee participation in corporate governance includes right to consultation on major company developments that may affect their livelihoods; collective bargaining; insisting on boards to consider the interests of other stakeholders, right to nominate or vote for supervisory board members where such are provided for, opportunities for employee share ownership and or profit sharing.

Right to consultation: Employees have right to be consulted on matters that affect their livelihoods such as workforce restructuring, plant relocation, reduction of working hours, introduction of job evaluation methods and changes in the company's legal status. This forces management to be more transparent in its dealings. This leads to more amicable working relations, reduces time spent on disagreements, reduces chances of collective job action, creates an open culture and makes management accountable for their every decision and action as employee buy-in would be needed.

Collective bargaining: This covers bargaining on pay, bonuses and general working conditions.

Boards to consider the interests of other stakeholders: Forces the board to be transparent its dealings with other stakeholders such as compliance with legal requirements and engaging in conduct that is socially acceptable especially for organizations operating in areas where there are strict social norms to be adhered to. Right to nominate or vote for supervisory board members where such are provided for: serves to place checks and balances on the actions of both management and the board. Employee share ownership and or profit sharing: enables employees to have board representation (some cases) – strengthening their ability to hold management accountable.

3.5.2. NGOs and Advocacy Groups

NGOs and pressure groups are part of corporate governance stakeholders as they tend to take action against those organizations deemed to violate acceptable practices (see Figure 3.5). For example, Greenpeace is an NGO focusing on environmental issues, World Wide Fund for Nature (WWF) focuses on wilderness preservation and reduction of human impact on the environment.

Greenpeace activists are arrested after storming cargo ship loaded with Volkswagen diesel cars off the Kent coast demanding VW takes its 'toxic' vehicles back to Germany

- The campaigners made their way next to the 23,498-tonne carrier, bringing Volkswagen cars from Germany , in the Thames Estuary in Kent this morning
- Activists hanging from the 89ft door and threatened to stay until ship turns back
- At Sheerness docks 40 Greenpeace volunteers scaled fences and gained access to the car park where thousands of diesel cars await collection from suppliers

http://www.dailymail.co.uk/news/article-4906110/Greenpeace-storm-ship-loaded-Volkswagen-diesel-cars.html

Asia Paper and Pulp (APP)

Greenpeace ran a campaign against paper and packaging giant, APP, by targeting the companies that were buying from it. One of the most high-profile actions against toy manufacturer Mattel focused on Barbie.

https://www.theguardian.com/sustainable-business/blog/greenpeace-campaigns-companies-lego-mattel-barbie-shell

Figure 3.5: Example of role of NGOs and Pressure Groups.

3.5.3. Customers

A firm's major customers influence its corporate governance as they may decide to boycott its products and or services if it is perceived as non-compliant with standards, guidelines and legal requirements. Customers increasingly want to be associated with suppliers with good corporate governance reputation.

3.5.4. Suppliers

Suppliers are a player in a company's corporate governance as customers both existing and potential have their buying decisions influenced by the sellers' products or inputs source markets. Where accompany is perceived as engaging in any form of unfair trade in its supplier chain this may result in the market rejecting its products. For example, organizations make it part of the corporate governance practices not to but from suppliers who use child labor, or are not to produce in an environmentally unfriendly manner, or whose production systems involve cruelty to animals.

3.5.5. Financial Markets

"Banks, for example, have played a governance role in their credit approval process and monitoring of corporate performance after a loan has been granted. However, as companies increasingly by-pass financial institutions and go directly to the debt markets, the markets themselves must provide the monitoring and discipline."

"We link corporate governance with liquidity, trading activity, and the clientele that holds the firm's stock. On the one hand, high liquidity can decrease the quality of a firm's governance because it reduces costs of turning over a stock attracting too many short-term agents who have little vested in good governance. On the other hand, liquidity can attract more sophisticated agents and hence improve the quality of a firm's governance. In our cross-sectional analysis, we find that high liquidity is accompanied by poorer governance and vice versa. Further, increased institutional holdings are surprisingly associated with weaker governance in the 1990s, whereas in later years, they are not significantly related to governance. The proportion of orders transacted by small (large) traders is associated with weaker (stronger) governance, supporting the notion that a clientele consisting of small, unsophisticated investors can weaken the discipline imposed by outside investors on management" (Subrahmanyam, 2008).

3.5.6. Community

The community in which a business is based is a major stakeholder in influencing corporate governance practices. Not adequately addressed or taken into consideration it can cripple the operations of an organization through for example boycotting its products and or services. Communities expect business to not only plough back some of their profits through corporate social responsibility initiatives but to also operate in a socially responsible manner by for example preserving the environment.

3.6. GOVERNANCE MECHANISMS

Mechanisms for corporate governance can be classified into two: internal and external controls. Internal mechanisms are those within the control of the company while external mechanisms are outside the direct control of the company.

CG internal controls mechanisms are meant to ensure efficiency in operations in order to achieve the desired results, ensuring that financial reports are reliable, and that there is compliance with relevant rules and regulations. They include:

- Strengthening shareholders' rights;
- Company structure;
- Company strategy;
- Board management monitoring;
- Executive Compensation;
- Compliance with internal controls;
- Independent risk and internal audit.

Figure 3.6 is an example of a company's public statement on internal control systems.

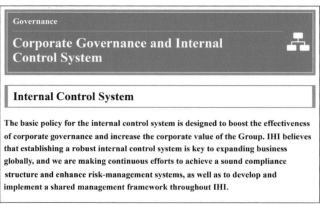

Figure 3.6: Example of statement on internal control systems. *Source*: http://www.ihi.co.jp/csr/english/governance/governance03. html#governance03_01.

3.6.1. Board Internal Monitoring

The board monitors the activities of management through insisting on compliance with regulations, financial reporting, operations efficiency and effectiveness, internal audit, remuneration and independent external auditors. Increasing complexity in the business environment has made it critical for Board of Directors to possess requisite specialist technical skills. Boards have found themselves having to acquire some specialist knowledge on matters within their areas of responsibility. Many boards have committees with smaller groups of directors with necessary knowledge and experience. Critical board committees through which closer supervision is carried out are the Remuneration Committee, Audit Committee and Finance Committee. In some instances boards have to hire consultants to assist their understanding of technical issues.

Part of Board monitoring is through appointment of the Chief Executive Officer (CEO) who works with the executive team to provide vision and leadership, and proposes the business strategy to the board and implements it once approved, and creates stakeholders' value in a balanced manner within the limits specified by the board. Accountable to the board, the CEO presents regular reports to the board.

The CEO is also responsible for succession planning for senior executives, assurance of business continuity in case of the loss of key managers, resolving any potential conflicts within the controlling family (if the company is owned or controlled by the family), sets the tone for workplace relations throughout the company.

3.6.1.1. Compliance with Internal Controls

Systems and procedures including reporting procedures such as financial reports, timely disclosure on material issues, functioning of internal audit without interference from the executives are some of the mechanisms used to track compliance with internal controls.

3.6.1.2. Independent Internal Audit

An independent internal audit department or section is a critical part of internal controls. In many companies the independence of internal audit is more theoretical than real. That at an administrative level internal audit reports to line management – specifically to the Chief Finance Officer (CFO) presents practical problems. There are many instances of CFOs interfering with the operations of internal audit to a point where the internal audit report only highlights issues passed by the CFO. Situations were internal audit reports to the CEO do not solve the problem either as information or audit reports reaching the board also tend to be managed by the CEO. Boards try to strengthen the independence of the internal audit through adopting an Internal Audit Charter that spells out the purpose, authority and responsibility of the function. An example of such a Charter is given in Figure 3.7. and Figure 3.8 is an example of internal audit failure.

Figure 3.7: Example of Internal Audit Charter Source: https://www.investec. com/.../Investec_group_internal_audit_charter_2015–16.pdf.

Toshiba - a case of internal audit failure
The 140-year-old pillar of Japan Inc is caught up in the country's biggest accounting scandal since 2011

Asish K Bhattacharyya
Last Updated at August 9, 2015 23:40 IST

Toshiba, a 140-year-old pillar of Japan Inc, is caught up in the country's biggest accounting scandal since 2011. In 2011, Olympus Corp was embroiled in a scandal. In July 2015, Toshiba Corp president Hisao Tanaka and his two predecessors quit after investigators found that the company inflated earnings by at least $1.2 billion during the period 2009-2014. Toshiba is one of the early adopters of the corporate governance reforms initiated in Japan. The corporate governance structure met corporate governance standards. Time and again cases of corporate governance failures have provided evidence that good corporate governance structure does not necessarily lead to good corporate governance. Organisation culture is a critical determinant of the quality of corporate governance.

Figure 3.8: Internal Audit Failure Source: http://www.business-standard.com/

article/opinion/toshiba-a-case-of-internal-audit-failure-115080900760_1.html.

3.6.2. Company Strategy

A company's strategy can serve as an effective governance mechanism as it provides the guidelines of the business' intended areas of emphasis over a given period. This works where the strategy is clearly articulated and performance measures that are a reflection of the strategy are put in place and monitored as illustrated in Figure 3.9.

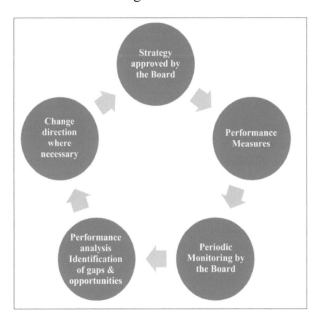

Figure 3.9: Strategy as an Internal Control Mechanism.

The key components of a company's strategic plan that serve as governance mechanisms are vision, mission, objectives, measures, company structure, and executive compensation.

3.6.2.1. Vision

The vision of the company spells out its desired destination. It is the responsibility of the Board to articulate a clear vision that serves as a guide for management. In reality in organizations it is management that proposes the vision. In SMEs the vision is held by the owner and may or may not be articulated in writing. For ease of holding management accountable and even the owner manager accountable it is better for a vision to be clearly articulated and documented. It serves as a guide. During the operations of the business challenges come and go and where a vision is not documented or articulated it is easy for an organization to end up drifting in a directionless manner. The vision therefore serves as radar or a pictorial view of the future state of the company. Big organizations grew out of compelling visions that were articulated while they were still small. The vision guides management's current and future action serving as the Boards ultimate guide for management. Management may change but the vision of the firm may not change as a result and therefore gives the firm continuity even the middle of management upheavals. That the Board provides the vision does not mean that management may not come up with a vision, however, this is subordinate and must be aligned to that provided by the Board.

Examples of Company Visions

Microsoft
Empower people through great software anytime, anyplace, and on any device.

Amazon
To be earth's most customer-centric company; to build a place where people can come to find and discover anything they might want to buy online.

Starbucks
To share great coffee with our friends and help make the world a little better.

Toys 'R' Us
To put joy in kids' hearts and a smile on parents' faces.

3.6.2.2. Mission

The organization's mission spells out why it exists, what it does, who it does it for and how it does it. It has four components which have to be clearly articulated by the Board to ensure continuity in the form of guidance provided to management:

- Core purpose – that clarifies the organization's reason to be;
- Values – the non-negotiable principles guiding the organization in all its operations;
- Customers – clear identification of who the organization servers or who its customers are
- Winning formula – how it serves.

Microsoft

Our mission is to empower every person and every organization on the planet to achieve more.

Starbucks

Our mission: to inspire and nurture the human spirit – one person, one cup and one neighborhood at a time.

Avon Mission statement is good example that captures a focus on benefits to all stakeholders (See Figure 3.10).

Avon Mission Statement

The Global Beauty Leader We will build a unique portfolio of Beauty and related brands, striving to surpass our competitors in quality, innovation and value, and elevating our image to become the Beauty company most women turn to worldwide. The Women's Choice for Buying We will become the destination store for women, offering the convenience of multiple brands and channels, and providing a personal high touch shopping experience that helps create lifelong customer relationships. The Premier Direct Seller We will expand our presence in direct selling and lead the reinvention of the channel, offering an entrepreneurial opportunity that delivers superior earnings, recognition, service and support, making it easy and rewarding to be affiliated with Avon and elevating the image of our industry. The Best Place to Work We will be known for our leadership edge, through our passion for high standards, our respect for diversity and our commitment to create exceptional opportunities for professional growth so that associates can fulfill their highest potential. The Largest Women's Foundation We will be a committed global champion for the health and well-being of women through philanthropic efforts that eliminate breast cancer from the face of the earth, and that empower women to achieve economic independence. The Most Admired Company We will deliver superior returns to our shareholders by tirelessly pursuing new growth opportunities while continually improving our profitability, a socially responsible, ethical company that is watched and emulated as a model of success.

Figure 3.10: Avon mission statement. *Source*: www.makingafortune.biz/list-of-companies-a/avon-products.htm.

3.6.2.3. Objectives

Objectives set for the executive team communicate what the Board considers important and is therefore willing to reward. Further, objectives motivate management to engage in specific behaviors. For good corporate governance objectives have to balance the interests of the various stakeholders beyond the profit motive.

3.6.2.4. Measures

Through the strategy both the Board and management can be held accountable but only if there are performance measures and mechanisms that facilitate performance reviews targeting all the areas considered as critical by the Board.

3.6.3. Company Structure

The way a company is structured in terms of reporting can be used as an internal governance mechanism. For example, should the CEO position be merged with that of Board chairman? How does that affect the independence of the Board? It is generally recommended that the position of chairman must be filled by an independent director as part of separation of leadership structure (Cadbury Report, 2003).

In theory organizations make decisions on reporting structures based on what they intend to achieve as per their strategic plan. The structure reflects the formal arrangement of jobs clarifying responsibilities and formal lines of authority and communication, compartmentalizing work to make responsibility boundaries clear. Further, the structure clarifies coordination of activities and facilitates clear allocation of resources making monitoring easier. It is the responsibility of the Board to ensure that the organization uses a structure that facilitates performance, monitoring and reporting. Mitsubishi built a reporting structure based internal control system to ensure legal compliance and compliance with the organization's Articles of Incorporation (see Figure 3.11).

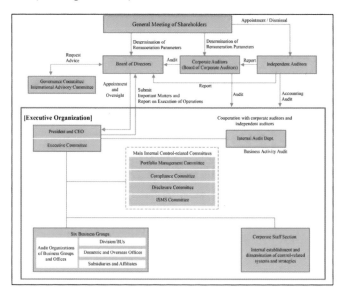

Figure 3.11: Mitsubishi Internal Controls. *Source*: www.mitsubishicorp.com/jp/en/csr/library/pdf/06sr-12.pdf.

3.6.4. Executive Compensation

Executives are expected to maximize shareholder value and in return get compensation usually in the form of a salary, a bonus that is related to annual business performance, business performance-based long-term incentives usually paid in shares. Strengthening corporate governance structures has been used as a mechanism for addressing agency problem relating to actions of executives. Increasing the ratio of independent directors on boards and strengthening remuneration committees responsible for handling executive pay have been used to ensure alignment between executive pay and company performance as a way of protecting the interests of shareholders. An example of a company's executive remuneration policy is illustrated in Figure 3.12.

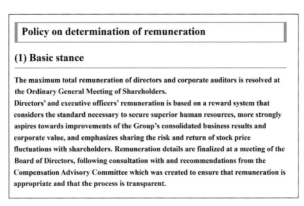

Figure 3.12: Executive Remuneration as an Internal Control Mechanism. *Source*: http://www.ihi.co.jp/csr/english/governance/governance01. html#governance01_02.

Empirical evidence, however, does not point to any major improvements that can be attributed to these measures (Ozkan, 2007). A number of factors explain this situation. Independent directors are not always independent because board members tend to be acquaintances of the CEO, who in most cases has some influence over their appointment (Murphy, 2012).

There is the problem of information asymmetry. Board remuneration committees usually do not have sufficient information to be able to make more informed decisions on executive pay. To address this deficiency they tend to rely on remuneration consultants who in fact are conflicted because of their other relationship with the Executives.

A desire not to be seen to be paying below the upper quartile of a perceived market, the remuneration committees tend to accept the recommendations of consultants with limited questioning. Empirical evidence has pointed to a situation where CEOs from the worst performing companies are paid most. Adams (2014) sites a study by Cooper, Gulen and Rau that demonstrates that:

- 150 companies with the highest paid CEOs were not performing well;
- as a group companies whose CEOs were in the top 10% in terms of pay posted the worst performance;
- the more CEOs were paid the worse their companies performed;
- at the top end of pay, the 5% CEOs who were the most paid posted results were their companies posted 15% worse results than their counterparts;
- the longer a CEO served the poorer was the performance of the company.

Directors do not necessarily represent the interests of the shareholder. An analysis of board remuneration actually points to yet another agency problem where the Board is also more inclined to serve the personal interests of its members to the exclusion of those of the shareholders (Murphy, 2012).

3.7. EXTERNAL CONTROLS

Other stakeholders who are main actors in corporate governance include customers, suppliers, local communities and government. A company's governance framework has to accommodate the interests of these other actors as if not properly handled could easily expose the company to reputation risk. These constitute the external corporate governance controls. The controls include:

- **Legal requirements:** businesses operate within legal requirements some of which are general applying to all businesses and others specific to a sector.
- **Government regulations:** In addition to the legal framework businesses are also subject to various government regulations and licenses, which may differ from sector to sector.
- **Profession bodies regulations:** Regulations developed by professional organizations both local and international for example accounting and auditing guideline, labor regulations such as ILO regulations, environmental standards relating for example to pollution and degradation, industrial product

standards, requirements for listing, and other reporting standards.

- **Financial reporting:** For public organizations there are requirements for specific financial reporting and for independent external auditors.

- **Transparency:** Requirements for disclosure are a control mechanism. OECD Principles of Corporate Governance have a requirement for timely and accurate disclosure on all material matters regarding a business; there is, however, controversy over what is material.

- **Institutional ownership:** Institutions exert performance demands from management which serve as a control mechanism in terms of minimum levels of performance.

- **Debt collectors:** The need to pay debtors controls any tendency towards low levels of performance that could result in failure to pay debts and present a threat to the business

- **Managerial labor market:** When there are limited jobs on the managerial labor market it serves as a control mechanism as executives cannot afford to be dismissed for poor performance or any other malpractice as chances of getting alternative employment would be minimal.

- **Media:** Attention from the media and possibilities of bad publicity serve as a check on executive performance as bad performance immediately finds its way to the public domain resulting in tarnished reputations and diminished respect from other stakeholders.

- **Competition:** The level of competition within a company's sector serves as a control mechanism. When competition is high intensives executives are forced to post high-levels of performance to survive.

- **Capital markets:** The markets present management and the board with the possibility of being a takeover target.

- **Pressure groups:** Non-governmental organizations and other pressure groups keep companies in check in areas that affect their operations. For example, environmental issues have forced organizations to adopt a more responsible ways of conducting their businesses.

A summary of external controls is presented in Figure 3.13.

Figure 3.13: Summary of External Controls.

3.8. SUMMARY AND CONCLUSION

This chapter identified key corporate governance actors as the shareholders, the board, management and other stakeholders. Mechanisms of corporate governance were identified as both internal and external to the firm. Internal mechanisms were described as those that fall within the control of the firm and include: the Board of Directors, management, independent internal audit, firm strategy and structure and internal reporting. External controls were identified as those outside the control of the firm and include: the legal framework and other regulations; pressure from non-governmental organizations; the managerial labor market; and public disclosure requirements. The next chapter deals with entrepreneurship with the intention of identifying elements of entrepreneurial firms that differentiate them from other forms of business and the implications this has for corporate governance mechanisms and practices.

QUESTIONS AND EXERCISES

1.   Identify and discuss internal corporate governance mechanisms.
2.   Identify and discuss external corporate governance mechanisms.
3.   Discuss different types and styles of Boards of Directors.
4.   Discuss the roles played by the key corporate governance actors.
5.   What role do pressure groups play in influencing corporate governance in organizations?

REFERENCES AND FURTHER READING

1. Aguilera, R. V., Desender, K., Bednar, M. K., & Lee, J. H., (2015). Connecting the dots: Bringing external corporate governance into the corporate governance puzzle. *Academy of Management Annals, 9*(1), 483–573.

2. Al-Janadi, Y., Rahman, R. A., & Omar, N. H., (2013). Corporate governance mechanisms and voluntary disclosure in Saudi Arabia. *Corporate Governance, 4*(4), 25–35.

3. Cossin, D., & Metayer, E., (2014). How Strategic Is Your Board?. *MIT Sloan Management Review, 56*(1), 37.

4. Hockerts, K. & Wüstenhagen, R., (2010). Greening Goliaths versus emerging Davids—Theorizing about the role of incumbents and new entrants in sustainable entrepreneurship. *Journal of Business Venturing, 25*(5), 481–492.

5. Ingley, C., Karoui, L., & Khlif, W. (2016) (November). Power Shift, Strategic Changes and Board Roles in SMEs: A Portfolio Approach. In *ECMLG 2016-Proceedings of the 12th European Conference on Management, Leadership and Governance* (p. 88).

6. Jenkins, H. & Yakovleva, N., (2006). Corporate social responsibility in the mining industry: Exploring trends in social and environmental disclosure. *Journal of Cleaner Production, 14*(3), 271–284.

7. Khlif, W., Ingley, C., Masmoudi, I. B., & Karoui, L., (2015) (October). Power Shifts and Board Roles in SMEs: A Multiple Case Study. In *ECMLG2015 – 11th European Conference on Management Leadership and Governance: ECMLG2015* (p. 167). Academic Conferences and publishing limited.

8. Murphy, K. J. (2013). Executive Compensation: Where We Are, and How We Got There. *Handbook of the Economics of Finance, 2*, 211-356.

9. Ozkan, N., (2007). Do corporate governance mechanisms influence CEO compensation? An empirical investigation of UK companies. *Journal of Multinational Financial Management, 17*(5), 349–364.

10. Peters, G. F., & Romi, A. M., (2014). Does the voluntary adoption of corporate governance mechanisms improve environmental risk disclosures? Evidence from greenhouse gas emission accounting. *Journal of Business Ethics, 125*(4), 637–666.

11. Scherer, A. G., Baumann-Pauly, D., & Schneider, A., (2013).

Democratizing corporate governance: Compensating for the democratic deficit of corporate political activity and corporate citizenship. *Business and Society*, *52*(3), 473–514.

12. Useem, M., (1986). *The inner circle: Large Corporations and the Rise of Business Political Activity in the US and UK*. Oxford University Press.

13. Zona, F., Gomez-Mejia, L. R., & Withers, M. C. (2018). Board Interlocks and Firm Performance: Toward a Combined Agency–Resource Dependence Perspective. *Journal of Management, 44*(2), 589-618.

4
CHAPTER

ENTREPRENEURSHIP

Chapter Aims and Objectives

This chapter discusses the entrepreneurship and governance-related characteristics of entrepreneurial organizations. By the end of the chapter you would have learned the following:

- Definitions of entrepreneurship
- Drivers of entrepreneurship
- Characteristics of entrepreneurial businesses
- The link between entrepreneurship and CG

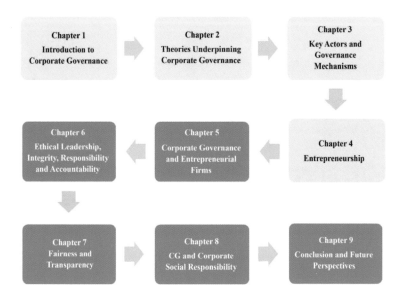

4.1. INTRODUCTION-ENTREPRENEURSHIP

Like CG, there are many definitions of entrepreneurship. Kuratko (2009) defined it as a dynamic process that involves the willingness to take calculated risk, assemble and direct necessary resources in pursuit of emerging opportunities where others see chaos. Ahmad, et al. (2010) defined it as involving recognizing opportunities, taking risk and being innovative with the intention of producing a profit. Schumpeter (1950 cited in Naudé, 2013) defined it as purposeful and systematic innovation while Gupta, MacMillan and Surie (2004) defined it as the process of constantly repositioning the organization to exploit opportunities in turbulent environments. What is clear is that the phenomenon is linked to identifying and exploiting opportunities out of otherwise adversarial conditions and taking advantage of loopholes in legislation and regulations.

There is therefore always an element of risk. For example, the regulator or legal framework could be amended to close the identified loophole. Entrepreneurship is accepted as a driver of economic progress through creating job opportunities and contributing towards development.

Definitions link entrepreneurship to exploiting opportunities in turbulent environments. Such environments present peculiar governance challenges as activities engaged in have legal, regulatory, societal and environmental implications. In many cases due to limitation of funds, time and knowledge entrepreneurs fail to act in a manner consistent with regulatory guidelines or generally accepted business practices. For example, taking risks goes beyond just financial risks to legal and societal risks as some of the opportunities they seize may either be in non-regulated areas or where regulation is not clear or where regulations have become redundant. In Eastern Europe and the Soviet Union 'grey' entrepreneurship exploited shortcomings in legislation and regulations by facilitating economic exchanges where none would have taken place and in that way took advantage of arbitrage opportunities (Peng, 2001). In situations where there is no or limited support for legitimate procedures for reaching business goals a situation is where unacceptable behavior (whether from a legal, societal or environmental perspective) becomes likely is created. While entrepreneurship depends on the government creating a favorable operating environment where there is stability, opportunities for business growth, and non-criminalization of entrepreneurial activities, absence of such support does not stop entrepreneurial businesses from emerging but rather facilitates the emergence of 'a dark side' of entrepreneurship that is dominated by poor CG.

An entrepreneur is someone who identifies a need and marshals resources to address the need and associated risks with the intention of realizing a profit. An entrepreneur therefore both establishes and runs a business – meaning ownership and management are both vested in the same person. McClelland, however, argues that an innovative manager who does not necessarily own the business can also be an entrepreneur. For our purposes the definition is limited to those who both own and run the businesses.

4.1.1. Entrepreneurship Theories

Casson's framework of entrepreneurship combines cultural and economic dimensions. Casson (2005) identifies entrepreneurship as critical to the growth and survival of companies operating in volatile environments and in that regard associates entrepreneurship with turbulent environments where decisions have to be made under complex circumstances.

Busenitz, Gomez and Spencer (2000) explain entrepreneurship in terms of three dimensions: regulatory, cognitive and normative. The regulatory component encompasses the legal framework, regulations, and state policies. These can either be supportive or non-supportive of the establishment of new businesses, moderate individuals' risk exposure as they start new businesses, and facilitate acquisition of resources. The cognitive dimension relates to business establishment knowledge people have within a country with some countries having more such knowledge than others. Normative dimension relates to the extent to which a society considers it normal or acceptable for people to engage in entrepreneurial activity or tolerates innovation and creativity.

Table 4.1: History of Entrepreneurship

Authority	Perspective	Views on entrepreneurship/entrepreneur
Ricardo	Economic	Type of skilled labor, entrepreneurs are providers of capital
Adam Smith	Economic growth	The 'invisible hand' that promotes economic growth through division of labor and market growth
Knight (2000)		The bearer of uncertainty whose return is pure profit
Schumpeter (2006)		Innovator and source of creative destruction
Casson and Kirzner		Coordination of transactions, intermediation, market making; pure profit is the reward
Metcalfe		Agents of self-transformation each responding to volatility created by activities of others
Licht and Siegel	Socio-cultural	Level and modes of entrepreneurial activities are related to culture and legal rules – entrepreneurs find ways of overcoming institutional deficiencies
Fogel, Hawk, Morck, and Yeung	Socio-cultural	Information gathering, processing, identifying arbitrage opportunities, risk-taking, market entry and start-up management, sourcing financial backing, acquisition of technological expertize. Subject to rent-extraction and outright asset grabbing

Source: Constructed from Casson, M., Yeung, B. and Basu, A. (eds.), (2008). *The Oxford Handbook of Entrepreneurship*. Oxford University Press on Demand.

4.1.2. Characteristics of Entrepreneurs

Entrepreneurs are distinguished by their ability to:

- Recognize opportunities;

- Having a drive to solve problems;
- Exercising innovation and creativity;
- Having initiative;
- Taking action regardless of impediments.

It is the last characteristic of entrepreneurs that usually find them operating in what can be termed as grey areas that may not necessarily be illegal but could be illegitimate, or even considered unethical, hence the expression "dark side of entrepreneurship."

There is often a gap between what some large groups in society consider to be legal as spelt legislated and regulated and what they consider legitimate as revealed in the customs, beliefs and values. According to Webb et al. (2009) when a large group defines what is ordinarily illegal as socially acceptable, for that particular group it becomes legitimate. The emergence of the informal sector is facilitated by this illegal-legitimate gap and most SMEs partly fall in this bracket where there are activities that can be classified as illegal but legitimate. These are differentiated from activities that are neither legal nor legitimate fitting the description 'renegade economy.'

Because entrepreneurs tend to operate at the boundaries of legality they experience problems in relating to what is accepted as ethical and unethical conduct. Unethical behavior is defined as that which contradicts the principles of what is considered right, honest or just. The environment and situation can affect an organization or entrepreneurs' unethical behavior.

Vaughan (1982) noted that when support for legitimate procedures to reach achieve goals are reduced the likelihood of participating in unlawful acts increases. In that situation a decision becomes unethical when its consequences have a negative effect on the interests of other groups. Fadahunsi and Rosa (2002) observed that among cross-border traders in Nigeria illegal practices were so rampant that they were the norm. Jong et al. (2010) noted that in situations where business conditions were antagonistic, entrepreneurs used bribery as a tool to counteract the challenges.

Entrepreneurs are usually SME owners although not every SME is owned by an entrepreneur. The difference between the two includes: attitude to amount of wealth creation, rate at which wealth is created, amount of risk taken and attitude to innovation. Table 4.2 below summarizes the differences.

Table 4.2: SME and Entrepreneurship

Dimension	SME	Entrepreneurship
Amount of wealth creation	Generate income that takes the place of employment	Substantial wealth going beyond what is personally need
Rate of wealth creation	Gradual	Rapid
Amount of risk taken	Low risk	High risk in anticipation of high returns
Attitude to innovation	Limited if any	High-levels of innovation

4.1.3. SME Defined

Definitions of an SME vary from region to region and even from country to country. Generally definitions are based on: number of employees, annual sales, total assets, total credit facilities and qualitative indicators. A third of economies in a survey undertaken by Kushnir et al. (2010) defined an SME as having less than 250 employees.

The examples below illustrate this point.

USA

Definition varies by industry guided by the North American Industry Classification System (NAICS). For example, in manufacturing an SME are those businesses with 500 employees or less and wholesale trades it is those with 100 employees or less.

Canada

Industry Canada defines an SME as those businesses with less than 500 employees. Small businesses are classified as those with less than 100 employees for goods-producing businesses and with less than 50 employees for service-based businesses.

European Union (EU)

The EU defines an SME as a business with less than 250 employees with those with less than 50 classified as small and those with less than 10 as micro. The EU also uses turnover as a guideline with the upper limit being EUR 50 million and the upper limit of size of balance sheet being EUR 43 million (https://stats.oecd.org).

UK

The UL has no standard for defining SME and the generally accepted guideline is that provided by the EU.

China

China's definition of SME varies by industry and is based on number of employees and or size of payroll, total assets and turnover (Figure 4.1).

Size Category	Industries	Employment-based	Total assets	Business revenue
Small	Industry	<300	¥40million	< ¥ 30million
	Construction	<600	¥40million	< ¥30million
	Wholesale	<100		< ¥30million
	Retail	<100		< ¥ 10million
	Transport	<500		< ¥30million
	Post	<400		< ¥ 30million
	Hotel & restaurant	<400		< ¥ 30million
Medium	Industry	300-2000	¥40million 400million	¥ 30million-300million
	Construction	600-3000	¥40million 400million	¥ 30million-300million
	Wholesale	100-200		¥ 30million-300million
	Retail	100-500		¥ 10million-150nillion
	Transport	500-3000		¥ 30million-300million
	Post	400-1000		¥ 30million-300million
	Hotel & restaurant	400-800		¥ 30million-150million

Note: SME meet one or more of the conditions. ME should meet three conditions. the are SE.

Figure 4.1: China SME categorization Source: Liu, X. (2008, p.39).

Africa

Throughout Africa there are various definitions with some countries using turnover of up to USD1 million as what constitutes SMEs.

The OECD defines SMEs as non-subsidiary independent businesses that employ less than a specified number of employees with the most frequently cited upper limit being 250 employees although a figure of 500 has also been used in some countries. That the SMEs come in different sizes means that their forms of corporate governance models cannot be generalized.

SMEs are not static. All or at least most entrepreneurial businesses start small with the intention of growing. At some stage they have to make decisions on form of incorporation, structure of organization, and even possibilities of public listing. With an eye on possible growth key questions the entrepreneurial business has to contend with are:

- How to access capital: building internal systems that make outside investors confident to put their money in the business.
- Fair return for the business owner: building systems that ensure that even as the business grows and outsiders invest in it the founder remains in control and gets a fair return for her efforts.
- Keeping innovation and opportunity seeking alive: as the business grows and 'formalizes' that it does not become overly bureaucratic and controls focused as to prevent it from quickly taking advantage of opportunities.

4.2. BARRIERS TO ENTREPRENEURSHIP

Entrepreneurs face a number of barriers most of which have implications for CG. Some of the barriers are:

- Cost of starting a business. Included in costs associated with starting a business are regulatory requirements;
- Property registration cost;
- Cost of export;
- Cost of import;
- Time needed for contract enforcement; and
- Legal and regulatory requirements.

4.3. CHARACTERISTICS OF ENTREPRENEURIAL COMPANIES

There are some characteristics that tend to be found in SMEs which have implications for CG. Some of the characteristics are products of the barriers and or challenges they face. Entrepreneurial businesses, at least during their early stages tend to have underdeveloped systems and procedures. These result in some of the following weaknesses:

- ***Poor financial management*:** record keeping is generally poor as in some cases personal expenditure is not separated from business expenditure, some labor costs, especially the owners' contribution are not accounted for, some costs go unrecorded or given the wrong accounting treatment and inventory management is generally poor.
- ***Limited or lack of experience*:** lack of exposure to other businesses

and contexts and lack of access to relevant advice results in poor decision-making, for example uncontrolled expansion driven by wrong assumptions.

- **Weak marketing:** this is compounded by use of unorthodox methods of marketing which if effective in the short-term may have adverse effects in the long-term due to their violating accepted business norms.

- **Poor risk management:** this could be in the form of miscalculated decisions, exposing the business to legal suits as a result of violations. This may also be driven by working from short-term horizons with limited consideration for longer term outcomes because of superficial understanding of the business or lack of strategic leadership or both.

- **Limited people management skills:** this usually results in labor problems, high rates of turn-over, inability to attract top notch talent and poor internal branding.

- **Absence of formal business planning:** this results in activities that are not synchronized, lack of long-term focus and risk exposure.

- **Poor business ethics:** the focus on survival and reaching profitability results in poor business ethics in many entrepreneurial companies. With poor concentrated in the owner or owners non-ethical activities have been found to thrive in such business setups. Ethics in business refer to practices and behaviors that are acceptable in the conduct of business in terms for example of discrimination, insider trading, false advertising, social responsibility, employer–employee relations, business relations with customers and suppliers, relations with the community and also among shareholders. Entrepreneurs have been found to be susceptible to unethical behavior.

Most entrepreneurial companies come in the form of family businesses. In that regard, the next section focuses on these.

4.3.1. Characteristics of Family Firms

Family businesses face risks and challenges that are different from those of non-family businesses. As a result they have specific characteristics over and above those generic to SMEs as listed below:

- •   Family plays a central role in leading and managing the business;
- •   There is an intention to transfer ownership to the next generation of the family;
- •   Family, business and ownership are all combined and interlinked;
- •   The owner has three roles: management, ownership and usually family head.
- •   A family-member owner not directly active in the management of the business retains influence as they represent long-term ownership.
- •   Non-owning family members who are active in the business also constitute part of the management structures.
- •   Non-family and non-owner-managers involved in the business, usually at a technical level.

4.3.2. Types of Family Businesses

Family businesses come in different forms such as: owner/operator, partnership, distributed, nested, and public (Baron and Lachenauer, 2016). Having an appreciation of the implications of each model facilitates having in place appropriate corporate governance mechanisms.

4.3.2.1. Owner/Operator model

This is the simplest model that keeps ownership in the founder(s). It has been used successfully by organizations such as Caterpillar who encourage their distributors to have an owner or one of the owners working directly in the business.

4.3.2.2. Partnership model

In the case of partnerships the leaders of the business are the owners who usually contribute equally in the business both in terms of time and finances and share the returns equally or based on some pre-agreed formula linked to one's contribution.

4.3.2.3. Distributed model

In this model ownership is distributed among several family members. Some of the family members work directly in the business while others are only owners. Those working in the business are usually remunerated separately from the returns their ownership related returns. In the absence of a clear governance structure this model is affected by disagreements between those family members who are working in the business and those who are not.

4.3.2.4. Nested model

In a nested model different branches of a family agree to jointly own some assets while also owning others separately so that within the larger family group there are smaller family groupings. The larger family group runs the business and distributes dividends to the smaller family groupings that may or may not in themselves run other businesses.

4.3.2.5. Public Model

In a public model a portion of shares are publicly traded so that they are not necessarily owned by family members. The business is ordinarily run by professional managers with the family focusing on representation on the board. However, some family members with the necessary expertize may also be involved in the day-to-day operations.

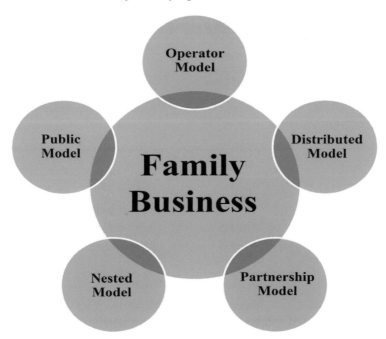

Figure 4.2: Family business models.

4.3.3. Governance Problems That Stand in the Way of Entre-preneurship Development

CG serves as both an enabler and a disabler of entrepreneurial activity in SME regardless of the ownership model. Reporting requirements and compliance issues can be burdensome especially in an environment where control mechanisms are not fully developed such as in emerging markets. For family businesses some corporate governance mechanisms leave the family with a perception of having lost control to professional managers who do not always act in the interest of the family's objectives. Some governance problems that have been cited as standing in the way of entrepreneurship are:

- Weak regulatory environment – a common feature in emerging economies;
- Lack of sustained government efficiency;
- Need for an entrepreneur to balance running the business with administrative compliance issues when there is no capacity to outsource as costs escalate.

4.4. ENTREPRENEURIAL COMPANY STAGES

Entrepreneurial firms go through stages in their development. There is the inception stage, growth stage, maturity stage, ossification stage and decline stage.

4.4.1. Inception Stage

The inceptions stage is largely characterized by trying to find capital, establishing the business, finding customers, recruiting staff and doing whatever is necessary to ensure existence. At this stage, the firm has few customers and weak contractual arrangements where customers call the shots as the firm pays the premium for being new and therefore without a track record. The firm at this stage is also exposed to suppliers and not in a position to negotiate favorable terms.

At this stage the company likely uses a simple minimum cost governance structure consisting of the founder or founders and a few if any employees. There is no separation in ownership and management. Decision-making is centralized and based on the experiences and knowledge of the founder. Employees are few, perform multiple tasks, are paid non-competitive rates, and most may be relatives or friends hired more for their perceived loyalty than a proven ability to perform. Those who are not have problems getting employment elsewhere and therefore have limited choices. Contracts of employment are verbal, if in writing they are not clear. In terms of reporting structures there is no formal packing order of jobs, no clearly stated areas of responsibility, and formalized lines of authority and responsibility boundaries. There are no internal governance guiding systems, custom and practice is what works. There is very limited focus on documentation and compliance with legislation and industry regulations. All powers in the organization are held by the owner who is accountable only to themselves and to legislative frameworks, which they may or may not necessarily adhere to. The owner plays all the governance roles played by the shareholder, the board, and management. Figure 4.3 depicts the inception stage of most entrepreneurial firms.

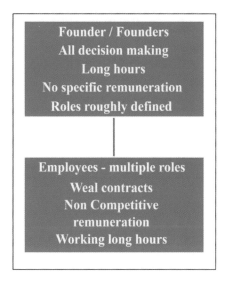

Figure 4.3: Firm structure at inception stage.

4.4.2. Growth Stage

In the growth stage the company focuses on finances, profitability, growth and hiring of more staff. Reporting structure is organic characterized by teams that are cross-functional and cross-hierarchical, free flow of information in an environment with wide spans of control, low formalization with decentralized decision-making. The openness of the structure makes it suitable for organizations operating in unstable environments there is still very little separation between the business and the owner. Systems remain weak but are being slowly developed in an attempt to formalize and overcome the burden of being new. While there may be some emergence of some departmentalization there is still no clear demarcation of responsibilities and lines of authority. The owner's role changes as they become less hands-on on some activities and starts playing an oversight role akin to that of shareholder and board. Figure 4.4 depicts this type of work structure.

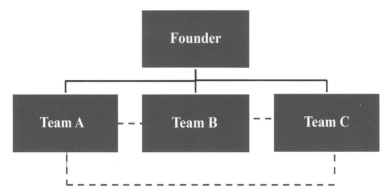

•No or weak formal systems
•Cross functional
•Cross hierarchical,
•Free flow of information
•Long work hours
•Multiple roles
•No clear demarcation of responsibilities and lines of authority

Figure 4.4: Growth stage structure.

4.4.3. Maturity Stage

At maturity stage the focus of the business is on strategy refinement, continued growth, managing success, refinement of systems and procedures, clarifying reporting structures, making wise investment decisions and institutionalization. At this stage the firm has become complex and the founder(s) may not have the capacity to take it forward. Responsibility is delegated to management marking the emergence of the agency problem although to a less extent than seen in public organizations, depending on the level of delegation and extent of separation of ownership from management. Decision-making is decentralized and this is reflected in the organization's structure having divisions and or clear functional areas. The company becomes more professional and introduces more stringent governance mechanisms to manage the complexity. The owner is less involved in the day-to-day running of the company, and may also not be involved in the oversight role as structures, systems and procedures are likely to be in place to ensure adherence.

The challenge for this company at this stage is to remain entrepreneurial in the face of increased formalization. The coming in of bigger investors dilutes the original owner shareholding transforming the business from an SME or alternatively the business fails to evolve and enters the pre-decline ossification stage. Figure 4.5 illustrates the structure in a mature entrepreneurial firm.

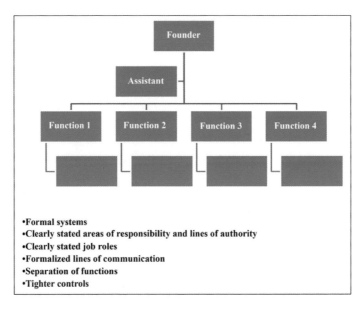

Figure 4.5: Mature entrepreneurial firm's structure.

4.4.4. Ossification Stage

The ossification stage is where the company has a stable equilibrium, systems are in place and have been institutionalized to an extent that when the business environment changes the firm fails to respond due to entrenched and non-flexible systems or processes resulting in absence of innovation leading to decline.

4.4.5. Decline Stage

At decline stage the organization has become a bureaucracy, high-levels of control, strict hierarchical communication, slow to respond to changes in the environment, little or no innovation and retrenching and closing some units.

Each one of the stages presents specific corporate governance challenges ranging from no attention to corporate governance issues at the inception stage to being paralyzed by corporate governance practices at the decline stage. Table 4.3 summarizes the issues.

Table 4.3: Summary of Firm Stages and Corporate Governance Implications

Stage	Major Activities	Corporate Governance
Inception	Finding capital Establishing the business Finding customers Ensuring existence Recruiting staff	No attention on governance Lower revenues therefore lower controls Owners, directors and management are the same people
Growth	Finances Profitability Growth – more recruitment Reporting structures Coping with growth – systems, etc.	Accounting policies Financial reporting mechanisms Internal Controls mechanisms
Maturity	Strategy refinement Continued growth Managing success Clarification of systems and procedures Wise investment decisions	Accountability of management Financial transparency Legal and regulatory compliance Independent directors Strong Audit Committee

Ossification	Institutionalized No innovation	Accountability of management Financial transparency Legal and regulatory compliance Independent technically competent directors Strong Audit Committee
Decline	Retrenchment Disinvestment	Shareholder rights – especially minority shareholders Employee rights

Figure 4.6 illustrates the relationship between the stage of a firm and the maturity of its governance structures. As the business grows to maturity, corporate governance structures tend to be strengthened as formalization increases. At decline stage they are likely to be weakened as the organization seeks to reconfigure itself in a changed environment where it once again finds itself in survival mode.

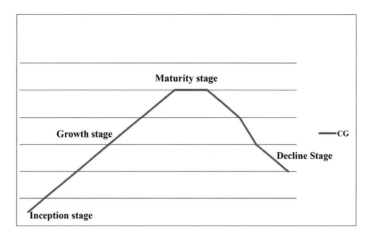

Figure 4.6: Relationship between Firm Stage and Maturity of Governance Structures.

Regardless of the stage of a business, there is a role for corporate governance. Benefits that SMEs could derive from corporate governance include:

• Having strategic direction as proper governance is partly premised on clarity of strategic direction, supporting strategic objectives and goals and tracking performance to ensure the achievement of the goals and eventually of the strategy.

- Enhanced leadership given that corporate governance demands for transparency, accountability, fairness and assurance exerts pressure on business leaders to engage in acceptable conduct.

- Improved decision-making resulting from awareness that whatever decisions a company makes are under public scrutiny in terms of their being consistent with the interests of the various stakeholders.

- Ability to monitor risks given that corporate governance results in improvement of company procedures, systems, processes and general financial reporting. The deliberateness of the processes makes it possible to identify risks and to address them.

- Gaining the confidence of internal and external shareholders: operating with increased measures of transparency makes both internal and external stakeholders have increased confidence in the organization. For example, employees become clearer on company policies and get a sense of practices being transparent and equitable. Potential investors are able to understand the company's current performance and therefore potential for future performance.

In SME the corporate governance structures have to be implemented in a manner that addresses the peculiarities of that form of business. There is no point in imposing governance standards of big corporations on an SME as they may be burdensome and result in their being reduced to a "box ticking" ritual as illustrated in the case in Figure 4.7.

> ***The Case of KBL***
>
> KBL Bank was set up by four young entrepreneurs in a developing country. Because of their educational background, all being educated to university level, and brief experience working in big banks they were all mindful of the need for corporate governance. As they set up their bank, which started off as a securities trading entity, they put in place a Board of Directors where they were all executive directors and also included five non-executive directors and a non-executive chairman.
>
> As the organization grew and set up subsidiaries in the form of an asset management arm, a stock broking arm, a merchant bank, a micro finance unit and eventually a commercial bank, they continued adhering to good corporate governance principles with each one of the entities having its own board dominated by independent directors. Even as the group proceeded to listing the business on the local stock exchange all the corporate governance practices were in place, so it seemed.
>
> After being in operation for 15 years and being praised as one of the success stories of opening up the banking sector to more players, the group started experiencing serious problems that culminated in its demise. A number of things seemed to have gone wrong and most of these pointed to corporate governance gone wrong. Among identified weaknesses were:
>
> - The Boards that seemed independent were in fact far from it as they were made up of friends, relatives and acquaintances of the founders.
> - The main founder who was the "owner" of the vision was overbearing and even made some decisions without consulting the other co-founders let alone the board;
> - As the business grew and posted significant profits the boards were increasingly reduced to rubber stamping bodies;
> - Non-performing insider loans were rampant;
> - The boards themselves were seriously conflicted as they also participated in insider loans;
> - Professional managers were forced to leave
>
> As the bank closed all its operations and employees found themselves jobless it became clear that – that a company has all corporate governance structures in place does not in itself mean that it is a good corporate citizen.
>
> **Discussion:** What could have gone wrong? Is it possible that right from the word go the governance mechanisms were never a part of KBL's daily practices?

Figure 4.7: KBL – When practices do not match what is on paper?

4.5. SUMMARY AND CONCLUSION

This chapter presented definitions of entrepreneurship and noted that though varied they all acknowledge that it involves elements of identifying and profitably exploiting opportunities and being innovative. It was also highlighted that in the process of exploiting opportunities and taking advantage of loopholes there may be legal and regulatory violations. Characteristics of entrepreneurial companies were discussed together with associated barriers and challenges. Characteristics of family firms were discussed given that most entrepreneurial firms are in fact family-owned. The relationship between the stage in which an entrepreneurial firm is at in terms of inception, growth, maturity, ossification and decline on the one hand and maturity of corporate governance mechanisms on the other was discussed. It was illustrated that inflexible entrenchment of controls can stand in the way of necessary innovation. This raises the question: What forms of corporate governance mechanisms are applicable to entrepreneurial firms? (Assuming entrepreneurial firms is synonymous with those SMEs and family businesses that are on a growth trajectory). The next chapter addresses this question.

QUESTIONS AND EXERCISES

1. Discuss the main characteristics of entrepreneurial firms.
2. Is entrepreneurship synonymous with absence of governance systems?
3. What forms of corporate governance mechanisms are applicable to entrepreneurial firms?

REFERENCES AND FURTHER READING

1. Acs, Z. J., & Szerb, L., (2007). Entrepreneurship, economic growth and public policy. *Small Business Economics*, *28*(2–3), 109–122.

2. Ahmed, I., Nawaz, M. M., Ahmad, Z., Shaukat, M. Z., Usman, A., Rehman, W. U., & Ahmed, N., (2010). Determinants of students' entrepreneurial career intentions: Evidence from business graduates. *European Journal of Social Sciences*, *15*(2), 14–22.

3. Backhaus, J. G., (2006). *Joseph Alois Schumpeter: Entrepreneurship, Style and Vision* (Vol. 1). Springer Science and Business Media.

4. Baron J. & Lachenauer T., (2016), The 5 models of family business ownership. Harvard Business Review.

5. Baron J., & Lachenauer R., (2016). The five models of family business ownership.   https://hbr.org/2016/09/the-5-models-of-family-business-ownership.

6. Busenitz, L. W., Gomez, C. & Spencer, J. W., (2000). Country institutional profiles: Unlocking entrepreneurial phenomena. *Academy of Management journal*, *43*(5), 994–1003.

7. Carney, M., Van Essen, M., Gedajlovic, E. R., & Heugens, P. P., (2015). What do we know about private family firms? A meta-analytical review. *Entrepreneurship Theory and Practice*, *39*(3), 513–544.

8. Casson, M., (2005). Entrepreneurship and the theory of the firm. *Journal of Economic Behavior and Organization*, *58*(2), 327–348.

9. Casson, M., Yeung, B. & Basu, A. (eds.), (2008). *The Oxford Handbook of Entrepreneurship*. Oxford University Press on Demand.

10. Fogel, K., Hawk, A., Morck, R., and Yeung, B., (2008). Institutional obstacles to entrepreneurship. In M. Casson, B. Yeung, A, Basu and N. Wadeson (Eds.), Oxford Handbook of Entrepreneurship. Oxford, UK: Oxford University Press. doi: 0.1093/oxfordhb/9780199546992.003.002.

11. Gupta, V., MacMillan, I.C. & Surie, G., (2004), Entrepreneurial leadership: developing and measuring a cross cultural construct. *Journal of Business Venturing, 19*(2), 241–260.

12. Hughes, P., (2017). How to run a successful family business. *Farmer's Weekly*, *2017*(17029), 30–30.

13. Ibrahim, B., Dumas, C., & McGuire, J., (2015). Strategic decision-making in small family firms: an empirical investigation. *Journal of Small Business Strategy*, *12*(1), 80–90.

14. Institute of Directors Sothern Africa. (n.d.). Governance in SMEs: A guide to the application of corporate governance in small and medium

enterprises.

15. Klapper, L., Laeven, L., & Rajan, R., (2004). Barriers to entrepreneurship. *NBER Working Paper, 10380.*

16. Knight, G., (2000). Entrepreneurship and marketing strategy: The SME under globalization. *Journal of International Marketing, 8*(2), 12–32.

17. Kumar, G. & Borbora, S., (2016). Facilitation of Entrepreneurship: The Role of Institutions and the Institutional Environment. *South Asian Journal of Management, 23*(3), 57.

18. Kuratko, D.F. & Audretsch, D. B., (2009). Strategic entrepreneurship: exploring different perspectives of an emerging concept. *Entrepreneurship Theory and Practice, 33*(1), 1–17.

19. Kushnir, K., Mirmulstein, M.L. & Ramalho, R., (2010). Micro, small, and medium enterprises around the world: how many are there, and what affects the count. *Washington: World Bank/IFC MSME Country Indicators Analysis Note.*

20. Licht, A. & Siegel, J., (2006). The social dimensions of entrepreneurship, in: Casson, M., Yeung, B., Basu, A. and Wadeson, N. (Eds.), *The Oxford Handbook of Entrepreneurship*, Oxford University Press, Oxford, 511–539.

21. Metcalfe, R., (2013). Can entrepreneurship be taught?. *Texas Education Review, 1.*

22. Morales, C. E., Holtschlag, C., & Marquina, P., (2015), January. Individual values, culture and entrepreneurship: Moving beyond a single level of analysis. In *Academy of Management Proceedings* (Vol. 1, 13091–13091). Academy of Management.

23. Naudé, W. (2014). Entrepreneurship and economic development: Theory, evidence and policy. In *International Development: Ideas, Experience, and Prospects*. Oxford University Press.

24. Peng, M.W. (2001), The resource-based view and international business. *Journal of Management, 27*, 803–829.

25. Smith, A., (2017). *The Wealth of Nations: An inquiry into the Nature and Causes*. Global Vision Publishing House.

26. Vandekerkhof, P., Steijvers, T., Hendriks, W., & Voordeckers, W., (2015). The effect of organizational characteristics on the appointment of nonfamily managers in private family firms: The moderating role of socioemotional wealth. *Family Business Review, 28*(2), 104–122.

27. Xiangfeng, L. (2007). SME development in China: A policy perspective on SME industrial clustering. *Asian SMEs and Globalization", ERIA Research Project Report, 5.*

5
CHAPTER

CORPORATE GOVERNANCE AND ENTREPRENEURIAL FIRMS

Chapter Aims and Objectives

Having noted that most entrepreneurial companies are family-owned and or SMEs, the extent to which what constitutes an SME differs from region to region and from nation to nation, what then are the governance issues relating to such enterprises? This chapter discusses the nexus of corporate governance and these enterprises. By the end of the chapter you would have learned the following:

- The general nature of corporate governance in entrepreneurial companies
- Benefits of corporate governance for entrepreneurial companies
- CG specific to SMEs and related challenges
- CG specific to family-owned businesses
- Examples of corporate governance in family businesses

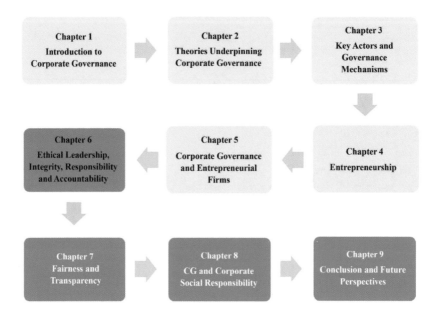

5.1. INTRODUCTION

CG is usually criticized for over concentrating on controls and compliance while ignoring performance a situation that works against entrepreneurial up-coming businesses. Partly because of its originating from seeking to control the owner-agent relationship, corporate governance mechanisms tend to be viewed as burdensome or even not implementable by owner-managers and family business. Businesses more often than not do not start big. Further, not every SME is family businesses neither are family businesses necessarily small or medium-sized. In fact, a number of big international businesses are in fact family businesses. The governance challenges they face will therefore vary as already illustrated, hence the need for corporate governance mechanisms that reflect the stage at which a business is at in its lifecycle. Further, founders of businesses have a significant influence on corporate governance systems in their organizations. Their influence is also determined by their own exposure and experiences with corporate governance. Businesses founded by professionals with previous corporate exposure are more likely to be mindful of some corporate governance practices than those founded by non-professionals with no past exposure to corporate life. Globalization and developments in communication technologies and opportunities to trade at an international level have increased pressure on

SMEs and or family businesses to adopt corporate governance frameworks that make them appealing to international suppliers, customers, investors and talent.

5.2. CORPORATE GOVERNANCE AND ENTRE-PRENEURSHIP CONUNDRUM

There are ongoing contradictions between corporate governance and entrepreneurship. Corporate governance focuses on preservation of the status quo in terms of corporate structure, systems, policies and procedures while entrepreneurship challenges the status quo through creative destruction. To that effect depending on the extent to which it is aligned to business objectives, corporate governance can aid or abate entrepreneurship (Eklund, 2014). Resolving the contradictions of corporate governance – entrepreneurship has generated much discussion (Thai et al., 2016). Some of the contradictions are:

- Who should play a leading role in the governance of the business? The entrepreneur or the professional managers?
- What role should the Board play? Should it focus on conformance or on performance?
- What relationship should the Board have with management? Is it supervision or support?
- What form of accountability must be in place? Should it be multiple or follow a specific chain of command?

5.3. ROLE OF BOARDS IN ENTREPRENEURIAL COMPANIES

Although governance structures in entrepreneurial companies may bear some resemblance to those in public companies, there are also major differences. The role of the Board in entrepreneurial companies, unlike in public ones, is not clearly defined as it is determined by the specific needs of the business. Forms Boards take include: affable; resource provider; prestigious professionals; and business lifecycle.

5.3.1. Affable Board

This form closely monitors and evaluates decisions made by management, is proactive and directly involved. The role-played is less supervisory as the members are part of the implementing team playing the role of coaching and advising. The success of the business hinges on the board playing its critical role. Although some members of the board could be outsider specialists in most cases they are qualified family members or owners of the business.

5.3.2. Resource Provider Board

This type of board focuses on facilitating access to resources and this is critical since SMEs are generally poorly resourced and lack capacity to access resources, markets, skills and networks.

5.3.3. Prestigious Professionals Board

Prestigious professionals in the relevant industry – improve acceptability of the company in targeted publics because of signaling value they bring in.

5.3.4. Business Lifecycle Board

The Board must be in line with where the company is in its lifecycle: inception, growth, maturity or decline.

What is critical, regardless of the form the board takes is for it to be driven by a high-level of chemistry, collaboration and mutual respect. Specific skills for Directors on an entrepreneurial company's board include:

- Having global strategic perspective;
- Widely read – too narrowness in skills does not cut it and can be expensive – as more people may be needed to make up for the skills gaps;
- Managerial courage to deal with especially successful entrepreneur owners – fearlessness in maintaining their independence;
- Quality of decisions that balance facts, experience, wisdom and sound judgment;
- Good intentions;
- Allocating sufficient time to their work including between meetings.

In dealing with corporate governance and entrepreneurship a distinction is made here between SMES and family businesses. It should, however, be understood that the two are not necessarily mutually exclusive.

5.4. KEY AREAS OF SME CORPORATE GOVERNANCE

When properly implemented corporate governance system ensures that the interests of the various stakeholders in an SME are considered. This is despite that at times such interests may be conflicting. International and regional organizations have provided some guidelines to SMEs in their respective areas which can be adopted and amended as necessary.

5.4.1. European Confederation of Directors Associations (ecoDa)

In Europe the European Confederation of Directors Associations (ecoDa) issued *Corporate Governance Guidance and Principles for Unlisted Companies in Europe* which are meant to guide businesses and their stakeholders (ecoDa, 2010). According to the guidelines for unlisted companies good corporate governance concerns putting in place a framework of value-adding organizational processes using a flexible gradual approach that considers factors specific to the organization such as level of openness and maturity, size and complexity. Figures 5.1 and 5.2 summarize the principles.

Phase 1 principles: Corporate governance principles applicable to all unlisted companies

Principle 1: Shareholders should establish an appropriate constitutional and governance framework for the company.

Principle 2: Every company should strive to establish an effective board, which is collectively responsible for the long-term success of the company, including the definition of the corporate strategy. However, an interim step on the road to an effective (and independent) board may be the creation of an advisory board.

Principle 3: The size and composition of the board should reflect the scale and complexity of the company's activities.

Principle 4: The board should meet sufficiently regularly to discharge its duties, and be supplied in a timely manner with appropriate information.

Principle 5: Levels of remuneration should be sufficient to attract, retain, and motivate executives and non-executives of the quality required to run the company successfully.

Principle 6: The board is responsible for risk oversight and should maintain a sound system of internal control to safeguard shareholders' investment and the company's assets.

Principle 7: There should be a dialogue between the board and the shareholders based on a mutual understanding of objectives. The board as a whole has responsibility for ensuring that a satisfactory dialogue with shareholders takes place. The board should not forget that all shareholders have to be treated equally.

Principle 8: All directors should receive induction on joining the board and should regularly update and refresh their skills and knowledge.

Principle 9: Family-controlled companies should establish family governance mechanisms that promote coordination and mutual understanding amongst family members, as well as organise the relationship between family governance and corporate governance.

Figure 5.1: Phased Approach Principles, Source: EcoDA (2010).

> **Phase 2 principles: Corporate governance principles applicable to large and/or more complex unlisted companies**
>
> **Principle 10:** There should be a clear division of responsibilities at the head of the company between the running of the board and the running of the company's business. No one individual should have unfettered powers of decision.
>
> **Principle 11:** All boards should contain directors with a sufficient mix of competencies and experiences. No single person (or small group of individuals) should dominate the board's decision-making.
>
> **Principle 12:** The board should establish appropriate board committees in order to allow a more effective discharge of its duties.
>
> **Principle 13:** The board should undertake a periodic appraisal of its own performance and that of each individual director.
>
> **Principle 14:** The board should present a balanced and understandable assessment of the company's position and prospects for external stakeholders, and establish a suitable programme of stakeholder engagement.

Figure 5.2: Phased 2 Principles, Source: EcoDA (2010).

5.4.2. United Kingdom

The Quoted Companies Alliance (QCA) in the UK developed Corporate Governance Code for Small and Mid-Size Companies (QCA 2013) while the country's Institute of Directors developed Corporate Governance Guidance and Principles for Unlisted Companies in the UK (IoD 2010).

According to the Institute of Directors UK, the bases of good corporate governance for unlisted companies in the UK, which can also be applicable to other regions are:

- Delegation of authority – as much as possible not having authority vested in a single office or person.
- Having delegated authority, to have clear checks and balances.
- Professional decision-making – decisions to be made guided by professional principles that and in the interest of the business as opposed to that of the owners.
- Accountability – for actions taken to ensure that the corporate good is served. Owner-managers tend to be found wanting in this area as they deem themselves as the ultimate authority in their business.
- Transparency – this is linked to being accountable to various stakeholders.
- Conflicts of interest – owners may not be able to separate themselves from the business to a point where their decision-making is compromised by their competing interests. For example, where they have to decide on disciplining a family

member employed in the business, or where decisions have to be made on giving family members loans.

5.4.3. Hong Kong

Hong Kong Institute of Directors developed Guidelines on Corporate Governance for SMEs in Hong Kong (Hong Kong Institute of Directors 2014).

5.4.4. International Finance Corporation (IFC)

IFC issued its *Family Business Governance Handbook* (IFC, 2011) that specifically addresses family-owned businesses and as already highlighted many of these are SMEs. The handbook provides guidelines on:

- Roles played by family members in a business;
- Importance of developing clear governance structures to guide the family;
- Board role, structure and composition;
- Role of senior managers; and
- CEO succession planning.

In formalizing corporate governance policies and procedures in SMEs a framework that incorporates the Board of Directors, establishing of internal controls, transparency and disclosure and shareholder relations is recommended.

Areas where a Corporate Governance Framework can Add Value to SMEs

From the guidelines provided by various organizations it is apparent that SMEs can derive value from having a corporate governance framework that emphasizes transparency, accountability and effective control. For example, the following can be realized from clarification of governance mechanisms:

- Enhancement of strategic decision-making, company's reputation, perceptions of trust from other stakeholders and in operations and productivity;
- Reduced conflict between among owners and between owners and management;
- Improved chances of accessing affordable credit;
- Faster business growth where desired;

- Protection from losses related to poor internal controls;
- Employee recruitment, retention and promotion;
- Transparent performance evaluation and compensation;
- Reporting and accountability structures;
- Discipline and grievance procedures.

Why SMEs may be Hostile to Corporate Governance Mechanisms

Given the benefits associated with having corporate governance mechanisms, why are SMEs generally hostile to them? There are a number of explanations. Implementing governance systems tends to gradually develop into a web of checks and balances that make the organization so bureaucratic that it fails to exercise creativity, innovation and entrepreneurship. Corporate governance structures in the form of a Board, Board committees, separation of duties, reporting mechanisms all have cost implications which are viewed as burdensome by SMEs especially when it is not clear what immediate value they would be adding to the business.

Even where some form of governance policies are in place, implementing them in a fair and equitable manner is not always possible, a situation which, in itself may create more problems in the workplace. This is particularly true for entrepreneurial organizations or SMEs where systems are still fluid and therefore subject to being amended on a regular basis.

There is also an inability to balance pressing business issues and less urgent governance matters and lack of understanding of how boards and independent non-executive directors contribute to business performance and. For example, SMEs generally view having a Board as a costly proposition. Having the right value-adding board members can, however, make the costs diminish in the face of accruing benefits. The Board can perform several functions such as provision of services and attracting resources to the business over and above exercising control and supervision.

Further, where an owner CEO manages to forego some measure of control by welcoming input from outside overall performance improvement can be observed. Involvement of outside directors has also been associated with provision on impetus for business growth and innovation.

5.5. CORPORATE GOVERNANCE IN FAMILY BUSINESSES

Family businesses are arguably the largest form of business in the world with about two-thirds of companies in the world falling in this category. Table 5.1 illustrates contribution of family businesses in different regions of the world.

The businesses have characteristics peculiar to them making them special cases for corporate governance purposes. Holderness and Sheehan (1988) found that among US companies those that are family-owned had a lower market value than the non-family-owned ones. Pérez-González (2001) found that the stock market reacted negatively when family heirs were appointed as managers while Villalonga and Amit (2004) reported that family control exhibited peculiar limitations where descendants constituted part of the executive team.

Table 5.1: Global Contribution of Family Businesses

Region	Contribution of companies that are family businesses
China	85.4% of China's private enterprises
Europe	60% of all European countries' turnover 40% – 50% of all employment
India	2/3 of GDP 90% of gross industry output 79% of private sector and 27% of overall employment
Middle East	Over 80% of businesses (except oil)
United Kingdom	25% of UK GDP
United States	50% of all companies 50% of listed companies

Source: http://www.ffi.org/?page=globaldatapoints

Family business governance presents more complex layers of relationships as the family members seek to balance multiple roles such as: owner, director, manager, employee, non-owner but employee family member and several other permutations. The businesses usually struggle to attract and retain professionals in their managerial positions. Corporate governance mechanisms are needed to clarify the relationship between professionals and family members particularly those put in managerial positions. During early stages of a family business there may not be any legal separation between business assets and family assets as family members tend to forego remuneration as they establish the business. Policies guiding corporate governance are limited and informal and there is a high reliance on a few people for decision-making rather than on any structures and processes which in most cases do not exist. This leads to:

- An amount of uncertainty and insecurity on the part of external investors and non-family employees;
- Weak internal controls that are tailored to the needs of the owners and their families
- Weak internal audit and financial accountability;
- Weak risk management partly as a result of clouded perspectives;
- Controls that lag behind company growth and business complexity;
- Unclear succession mechanisms.

Despite corporate governance flaws, the competitive advantage of family-controlled companies has been linked to their system of corporate governance that ensures that the family has control rights over the business assets. This constitutes a source of competitive advantage when resources are scarce as they facilitate use of social capital and exploitation of emerging investment opportunities and innovation. The family that owns the business typically assumes the leadership position. In such a situation the family, the ownership group and the business all need governance. Where the governance framework is in place there is clarity of roles, rights and responsibilities among the three: family, ownership and business. All the three parties act responsibly within the confines of their mandates and there is appropriate involvement of the family and ownership in the business. The governance framework provides for:

Clear articulation of the business vision, mission and overarching objective(s);

- Clear articulation of the roles of shareholders directors or advisors, management and how they all relate in terms of procedures and limits of authority;
- Clear succession planning process for both management and ownership levels;

• Mechanisms for transparent information dissemination and sharing among shareholders and with other stakeholders.

5.5.1. Governance Structure

Governance structures of family businesses vary based on business size and diversity, diversity of the family and the generation of the owners. For example, there could be a first-generation business where an owner manager has 100% ownership of the business. There could also be a second generation business where there is the family owner manager holding a large portion but not 100% of the shares but serving as CEO and in that regard holding the positions of being both a principal and an agent. There could also be a third and other subsequent generation family business where family are only principals and not agents meaning the family business then has to deal with agent problems found in public companies. At this stage family members are not directly involved in the management of the business but exercise their control through the Chairman of the Supervisory Board. In such situations corporate governance issues do not necessarily relate to the relationship between the Board and Ownership and the Board and management or to compliance issues but rather to ensuring that the business has processes and procedures and systems that guarantee its sustainability. Figure 5.3 presents examples of leadership challenges faced in family businesses.

Figure 5.3: Leadership Challenges in Family Businesses. *Source*: https://hbr. org/2015/04/leadership-lessons-from-great-family-businesses.

The exact corporate governance mechanisms ideal for spurring economic growth vary across geographical and national locations and governance systems which affect business governance practices. They therefore remain unresolved. That notwithstanding, governance structures ordinarily applicable to family businesses are:

- Executive management consisting of the group's top management, included here is the question of ownership and management succession.

- Board of Directors or Board of Advisors responsible for ensuring company sustainability, hiring and retaining qualified professionals. While it is necessary to match numbers of family members on the board with non-family members, this must not be at the detriment of the benefits the business derives from being a family business.

- Family Council that deals with policies on family involvement in the business including family employment policies; clarification of relations between family salary-earners and family dividend-receivers; and intra-family decision-making processes;

- Shareholders meeting.

In Singapore, PWS (2016) identified corporate mechanisms recommended for family businesses in that environment (Figure 5.4). The mechanisms mirror those of public companies but are adjusted to suit family business circumstances.

Mechanism	Equivalent in Public Company
Family Constitution - set of rules governing relationships	Company's Articles of Association
Family Council	Board of Directors
Annual Family Meeting	Annual General Meeting
Sub-committee of family council to handle disputes	Board sub committees
Handing over to next generation	Structurd succession planning
Acceptance of non family critical skills	Diversity and talent managemet

Figure 5.4: Governance of Family Businesses – Singapore. *Source*: Adapted from PWC (2016). Successful Family Businesses: Generation after generation.

5.5.2. Benefits for Family Business

Motivations for improving governance policies and practices in family-owned businesses include:

- Facilitation of the implementation of the business strategic plan;
- Need to formalize the business model and or strategy and ensure that it is sustained;
- Enhancement of shareholder value and the attractiveness of the business to outside investors;
- Improve ability to attract specialist professionals as part of the business talent pool;
- Facilitate access to global markets and investors; and
- Enhancement of company image both locally and internationally.

According to OECD the quality of a company's corporate governance affects its long-term development. The continuity of a family business beyond its founding members is dependent on the quality of its corporate governance. Successful family businesses are those that while recognizing the power of their ownership control, voluntarily put in place an independent board and clearly defined roles and responsibilities for the owners, management and the board. Once such mechanisms are in place the family businesses is able to pursue unconventional strategies, the family can be an agent for faster and effective decision-making; the company is able to handle those elements of traditional corporate governance that stifle entrepreneurship and innovation; transparency and partnership among the stakeholders is enhanced and good performance is sustained. Table 5.2 presents examples of some successful family businesses and their corporate governance mechanisms or structures.

5.5.3. Examples of Successful Family Businesses and Their Corporate Governance Mechanisms

Table 5.2: Examples of Successful Family Businesses

Business	Governance
Sun Pharmaceutical (India)	Founder remains the largest shareholder
Carnival Corporation USA	Micky is Chairman and a former CEO of Carnival
Phillips 66 USA	Phillips family has remained large shareholders in the company.

Reliance Industries India	Family serving as Chairman and CEO Another three family members sit on the boards
Richemont Switzerland	Founding family retains major shareholder
Sun Hung Kai Properties Hong Kong	Family holds board chairmanship, board positions and top management positions
McKesson USA	Significant amount of shares are still held by founding family
SoftBank Japan	Family in CEO position
Tata Consultancy Services India	Promoter and major shareholder retains control
Nike USA	Family have board seat, up to 2016 founder chaired the board
Volkswagen Germany	At least five family members sit on the board
Samsung Electronics	High family involvement at both board and top management level; corporate governance problems have been sited
Oracle USA	Board chaired by the founder for a long time
Facebook	Family involved in business – board and management
Walmart – USA	Family sit on the company's Board of Directors and also occupy the chairmanship
Roche – Switzerland	Family controls the company through their voting pool.
Norvatis Switzerland	Family Foundation is the company's single largest shareholder and its president sits on Board of Directors

Source: Source: http://www.businessinsider.com/the-worlds-21-biggest-family-owned-businesses-2015-7.

5.6. CORPORATE GOVERNANCE CONTROVERSIES

Successful family businesses have not been immune to corporate governance-related controversies showing that having a corporate governance framework in place does not in itself result in adherence to the articulated practices illustrating that corporate governance problems are not only limited to the less successful or to the smaller entrepreneurial companies as illustrated by the examples below.

5.6.1. Case of Samsung Case

MARCH 11, 2016 by: Song Jung-a in Seoul

Samsung Electronics faced shareholders disgruntled over the company's deteriorating performance and governance problems at its annual general meeting on Friday.

The meeting, packed with 400 individual and institutional investors, lasted for more than three hours and featured an unusual vote on the appointment of board members.

Proceedings were frequently interrupted by vocal shareholders raising concerns about issues including the company's slowing growth, lack of new growth drivers, and poor oversight by outside directors.

It marked a change from the annual meetings commonly full of praise for the South Korean company's performance that typically concluded within an hour.

Friday's unruly proceedings highlighted growing assertiveness from domestic shareholders, who have been traditionally passive in the face of firm family control and opaque decision-making.

However, restless investors made their presence felt by opposing the reappointment of two board members — JK Shin, in charge of the mobile business, and Yoon Bookeun, head of consumer electronics — and demanding measures to revitalise the slowing smartphone business and boost low margins for home appliances.

Shareholders also opposed the appointment of several outside directors whose independence they questioned. "Outside directors are still acting as rubber stamps on company policies. How can we expect quality oversight by them against management decisions against shareholder interests?" complained one shareholder.

Experts expect Samsung to face growing pressure for a corporate governance overhaul.

"The good old days are over. The AGM will no longer proceed according to Samsung's scenario," said Kim Sang-jo, economics professor at Hansung University. "Shareholders, unhappy with the company's performance, will no longer put up with governance problems."

Figure 5.5: Samsung corporate governance Challenges, *Source*: Jung-a, (2016). Tempers fray at Samsung electronics AGM. https://www.ft.com/content/ed6cc15e-e757-11e5-ac45-5c039e797d1c.

5.6.2. Walmart

In spite of having a clear statement on corporate governance practices (Figure 5.6) Walmart has been caught up in corporate governance misdemeanors, such as:

- The bribery storm in Mexico in 2012 (*https://corpgov.law. harvard.edu/.../Walmart-bribery-case-raises-fundamental-governa...*);
- Exploitation of workers and an anti-union attitude;

- Non-independence of so-called independent directors and conflict of interest (http://www.huffingtonpost.com/al-norman/walmart-at-50-a-crisis-of_b_1489776.html).

Figure 5.6: Walmart Corporate Governance Statement. *Source:*   .

An organization's corporate governance intentions are not always reflected in practice making corporate governance principles seem more academic than practical. In reality businesses are focused on managing the environment, competition and other factors with adherence to governance issues coming in as an after-thought – it would seem. This may be indicative of the evolving, contextual and situational nature of corporate governance practices. A mechanism that may work well in one situation may not work in another, thus what is documented as the corporate governance policy is not necessarily what is practiced. Further, people have different views on what is acceptable corporate governance as what an organization claims to be its corporate governance practices and or guidelines as reflected in annual reports varies with opinions of third parties as is reflected in the Walmart case. One of the reasons being the way corporate governance is increasingly viewed as including an element of corporate social responsibility.

5.7. SUMMARY AND CONCLUSION

This chapter covered the general nature of corporate governance in entrepreneurial companies, benefits of corporate governance for entrepreneurial companies, corporate governance challenges specific to SMEs, practices in family-owned businesses and presented examples of corporate governance practices, successes and failures in family businesses. What is clear is the role of the founders and families in the corporate governance of entrepreneurial firms. This is in sharp contrast to the situation observed for public companies highlighting the need for a corporate governance framework that is amicable to SMEs and owner or family run enterprises. The next chapter focuses on ethical and effective leadership and responsibility and the next three chapters focus on the other three aspects of corporate governance in SMEs.

QUESTIONS AND EXERCISES

Case Study: 2 Sisters – Was It a Slip in Corporate Governance?

Read on the 2 Sisters scandal reported in The Guardian sources indicated below.

Company background information:

- The Board has four executive directors two of which are the owners and founders of the business; five non-executive directors one of which is the chairman, and another is classified as a senior independent director.

Figure 5.7: History of 2 Sisters, Source: Adapted from http://www.2sfg.com/about-us/how-we-work/ethics/.

Figure 5.8: Is it a slip in corporate governance? *Sources*: https://www.the-guardian.com/business/2017/sep/28/uks-top-supplier-of-supermarket-chicken-fiddles-food-safety-dates, https://www.theguardian.com/business/2017/oct/01/scandal-hit-2-sisters-suspends-chicken-production-at-west-midlands-plant, https://www.theguardian.com/business/2017/oct/03/2-sisters-west-bromwich-chicken-plant-foodroup.

1. Identify and discuss pertinent corporate governance issues in the story.

2. Corporate Governance is more an academic than a practical concept. Discuss this statement by giving examples to support your views.

3. Adhering to all principles of Corporate Governance can be detrimental to business performance. Discuss this statement by giving examples to support your views.

4. Entrepreneurship and Corporate Governance as practiced in public companies are not compatible. Discuss this statement by giving examples to support your views.

REFERENCES AND FURTHER READING

1. Baron J & Lachenauer T., (2016). The 5 models of family business ownership. Harvard Business Review.

2. Bennedsen, M., Fan, J. P., Jian, M. & Yeh, Y. H., (2015). The family business map: Framework, selective survey, and evidence from Chinese family firm succession. *Journal of Corporate Finance*, *33*, 212–226.

3. Eklund, J., (2014). *Corporate Governance, Entrepreneurship and Economic Development. Swedish Entrepreneur Forum* (No. 28). Working Paper.

4. Falkner, E.M. & Hiebl, M. R., (2015). Risk management in SMEs: a systematic review of available evidence. *The Journal of Risk Finance*, *16*(2), 122–144.

5. Ha, T. T., Chau, N. N., & Hieu, N. T., (2016). The Impact of Governance on Entrepreneurship Development in ASEAN+ 1 Countries: Evidence from World Bank Datasets. *Modern Economy*, *7*(5).

6. Heineman, B., (2012). Walmart bribery case raises fundamental governance issues. *https://corpgov.law.harvard.edu/.../Walmart-bribery-case-raises-fundamental-governa...*

7. Huse, M., (2007). Boards, governance and value creation: The human side of corporate governance. Cambridge University Press.

8. Jung-a, S., (2016). Tempers fray at Samsung electronics AGM. https://www.ft.com/content/ed6cc15e-e757-11e5-ac45-5c039e797d1c.

9. Pérez-González, F., (2001). Does inherited control hurt firm performance. *Unpublished Manuscript. Columbia University*.

10. Pinheiro, R., & Yung, C., (2015). CEOs in family firms: Does junior know what he's doing?. *Journal of Corporate Finance*, *33*, 345–361.

11. Shadab, H. B., (2007). Innovation and corporate governance: The impact of Sarbanes-Oxley. *U. Pa. J. Bus. and Emp. L.*, *10*, 955.

12. Singla, C., Veliyath, R. & George, R., (2014). Family firms and internationalization-governance relationships: Evidence of secondary agency issues. *Strategic Management Journal*, *35*(4), 606–616.

13. Smit, Y. & Watkins, J. A., (2012). A literature review of small and medium enterprises (SME) risk management practices in South Africa. *African Journal of Business Management*, *6*(21), 6324.

14. Stacchini, M. & Degasperi, P., (2015). Trust, family businesses and financial intermediation. *Journal of Corporate Finance*, *33*, 293–316.

15. Team T., (2012). Knight Capital is just another example of poor risk management. https://www.forbes.com/sites/greatspeculations/2012/08/03/knight-capital-is-another-example-of-poor-risk-management/#631ae1ed17a4.

16. Thun, J. H., Drüke, M. & Hoenig, D., (2011). Managing uncertainty–an empirical analysis of supply chain risk management in small and medium-sized enterprises. *International Journal of Production Research, 49*(18), 5511–5525.

17. Villalonga, B., Amit, R., Trujillo, M. A., & Guzmán, A., (2015). Governance of family firms. *Annual Review of Financial Economics, 7*, 635–654.

18. Villalonga, B., Trujillo, M. A., Guzmán, A., & Caceres, N., (2017). What Are Boards For? Evidence from Closely Held Firms. *CESA School of Business*.

19. Xiangfeng, L., (2007). SME development in China: A policy perspective on SME industrial clustering. *Asian SMEs and Globalization", ERIA Research Project Report, 5*.

6
CHAPTER

ETHICAL LEADERSHIP, INTEGRITY, RESPONSIBILITY AND ACCOUNTABILITY

Chapter Aims and Objectives

CG in SMEs hinges on ethics and integrity, effective leadership that is responsible, accountable, fair and transparent. This chapter focuses on the first three aspects. By the end of the chapter you would have learned about the following:

- Ethics, integrity and corporate governance interface;
- Benefits of ethics to business;
- Responsibility as reflected through:
    - Strategic planning and implementation;
    - Developing supportive structures; and
    - Managing organizational change.
- Accountability as reflected through:
    - Company compliance with relevant legislation;
    - Risk management;
    - Business continuity;
    - Succession planning.

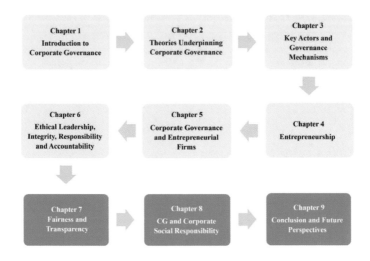

6.1. INTRODUCTION

Clearly there is no universally accepted model of corporate governance for entrepreneurial companies, in this instance SMEs and family businesses. That notwithstanding, there are basic pillars of corporate governance for SMEs regardless of individual peculiarities. Further, professional organizations have provided guidelines that can be amended and used as found fit.

Figure 6.1: Ethics and integrity in SME governance.

In discussing the case of corporate governance in SMEs, Cadbury's (1992) definition of corporate governance as the system used to direct and control companies is most appropriate. Given that definition, in SMEs corporate governance is premised on systems that are based on ethical and effective leadership that is responsible, accountable, fair and transparent (Figure 6.1).

6.2. ETHICAL LEADERSHIP AND INTEGRITY

At the center of corporate governance for SMEs is ethical leadership and integrity. Among factors that influence clients' reluctance to engage in business with SMEs is a general view that most are not ethical, have no integrity, are fly by night businesses and therefore cannot be trusted. In fighting the liabilities of being new and or being small is the need to demonstrate being ethical and having integrity.

Ethics are a major challenge for entrepreneurial leaders. Decision-making by entrepreneurial owners is guided by factors that go beyond extant legal guidelines as they at times work in new areas where there are either no guidelines or legal frameworks or where the guidelines are inadequate. In such situations the entrepreneurial leader's value system becomes a critical guiding component in making business decisions. Such leadership is susceptible to unethical behavior because of the strong dependence of the followers on the leader's guidance.

Two ethical theories used in business literature are utilitarianism and deontology. According to deontology acts are classified as either good or bad regardless of their consequences. Utilitarianism on the other hand is hinges on an assessment of the rightness or wrongness of an act based on its results bringing more good or more evil so that no decision and or act is inherently wrong or right.

Table 6.1: Summary of Deontology and Utilitarianism

Deontology	Utilitarianism
Emphasizes one's duty to do a certain action regardless of the results of that action Focus is on the principle – laws, regulations, rules, codes of conduct, etc. without regard for the consequences	Maximizing everyone's benefits – therefore the greatest good for the company and its employees is to maximize profits. Universal acceptance – if one's actions are in accordance with the general principles and their desired outcomes then one's actions are ethical

6.2.1. Ethics Are Contextual

Ethics are contextual and situational. In reality when the survival of an entrepreneur's business is threatened they rarely find the time to evaluate the ethical acceptability of a decision. According to Bennington (2000) issues of ethics emerge in situations where a case does not fit into existing rules so that a decision has to be made in the absence of a guiding framework. It is a dilemma. This is compounded by what was observed by Webb et al (2009) that because of the gap that often exists between what is considered to be legal as captured laws and regulations and common practices, beliefs and values there are situations where a dominant group accepts what is defined as illegal as socially acceptable making it legitimate to that group.

This gap between what is legal and what is legitimate creates conditions for the emergence of an 'informal' economy of illegal yet legitimate activities. Such an economy includes some activities that have no legal support and no social acceptance and are considered as constituting a renegade economy. Clearly environmental factors affect the possibility of the occurrence of unethical behavior and therefore unethical leadership. Where there is lack of support for legal and legitimate procedures to reach goals illegal and or illegitimate activities thrive as the entrepreneurs will not suspend their entrepreneurial activities but will find a way out of a perceived impediment in order for their ventures to survive. In some transitional economies illegal practices are the norm and operate as a parallel economy with its own traditions and values. They offer entrepreneurs ways of achieving their goals in situations where there is no alignment between society's goals and approved procedures of pursuing goals hence Jong, Tu and Ees (2010) argument that bribery, a vice, offers entrepreneurs a way of counteracting antagonistic business conditions.

When the environment has uncertainties or has many external threats, what are considered as ethical standards become unclear as business owners and their employees are more likely to tolerate levels of unethical conduct they feel works in the interest of the business. When there is turbulence in the environment or an organization is in transition or where there is conflict and uncertainty ethical leadership can be compromised. For example, Barneji and Krishnan (2000) found that transformational leadership while good for organizations in transition did not always raise the ethical aspirations of a group.

There is a clear clash between ethical leadership as conceptualized from a good corporate governance perspective and the realities entrepreneurs face on the ground. It is on that basis that entrepreneurs shy away from having boards that could pause as a limiting factor to their context sensitive decision-making. Where the ethical leadership component of corporate governance is concerned one of the main issues to be addressed is achieving balance between efficiency and effectiveness. For as long as corporate governance is deemed as an impediment to entrepreneurial decision-making and as a creation of a dominant group labeling the activities of the less powerful as illegitimate, illegal and anti-social, the schism will persist.

6.2.2. Benefits of Ethics to Business

Notwithstanding controversies on ethics, it is accepted that good ethics is good business indicating that a business has more to gain from being perceived as ethical. Some benefits of ethics to business are:

- Customers feel more comfortable conducting business with a company they perceive as ethical;
- Perceptions of risk in doing business with the company are minimized;
- There can be financial benefits, for example in attracting funding;
- Positive influence on the moral behavior of employees and;
- Using company reputation for ethics strategically by embracing it as an integral part of the company's brand and a source of competitive advantage.

Corporate governance structures help to portray an organization as ethical and as having integrity to other stakeholders who are not necessarily the shareholders. Ethical conduct and integrity are reflected in the organizations decisions and action and also in the processes or deliberations that lead to the decisions and actions. Having clearly defined vision, mission and organizational values backed by supportive systems and processes reduces the likelihood of unethical behavior. Spelling out values and making them transparent to even external stakeholders guards the organization against, for example, environmental and social violations as the organization will continuously seek to align its decisions and actions with its espoused purpose and values, to act in a manner perceives as fair and to be accountable to all its stakeholders.

6.3. RESPONSIBILITY

Being responsible in terms of SME corporate governance hinges on the subsistence of a clear strategy, developing supportive structures which include reporting structures, configuration of jobs, managing whatever changes are necessary for the realization of business objectives and planning for business continuity.

6.3.1. Strategy

Business strategic planning is used in bigger organizations as part of the monitoring component of corporate governance. Most SME and entrepreneurial organizations tend not to engage in formal strategic planning preferring the back of envelope approach as explained by Branson of Virgin (Figure 6.3). Where planning takes place it has been found to be characterized by: shorter time horizons, low level of formalization of the process, less use of standard strategic planning frameworks, and limited control and follow up mechanisms.

In an SME set up strategic planning addresses the "responsible" part of SME corporate governance. Granted the process may not be as detailed as that found in large organizations but nevertheless have the key components to address issues of the business' purpose and values and must guide the appropriate allocation of resources. Coming up with the strategy forces business owners to consider risk indicators and conditions in the organization's internal and external environment. This enables the owners to consider the interests of other stakeholders and the way these could impact on the business both in the short and long-term. For example, it would be irresponsible for the business leaders to focus on short-term gains, which could expose the business to future risks as a result of legal action or being perceived as socially or environmentally irresponsible. The existence of a documented strategy therefore ensures that there is a template that forces actors to engage in activities that result in sustainable outcomes that help the business grow. Further, it makes it possible to make management accountable for stated objectives. To that effect embarking on formal strategic planning is one of the critical components of holding both owners and management within the SME responsible. Although the strategic planning process in big organizations can be elaborate and expensive, this does not mean that SMEs cannot undertake the process. Some authors have argued against SMEs spending resources on formal strategic planning preferring that they have a more flexible approach (Mintzberg, 1993). This view implies that formal

strategic planning does not accommodate flexibility, which in fact is not the case. More recent studies have indicated the absence of any differences in financial performance between SMEs that engage in formalized and well documented strategic planning and those who do not, again suggesting that strategic planning is not appropriate for SMEs, at least not in the format in which it is practiced in bigger organizations.

Some of the reasons for shunning formal strategic planning in SMEs are:

- Lack of human resources are kept at the minimum possible levels which means they are stretched and not available to participate in lengthy strategic planning sessions.

- Knowledge of broad management issues including strategic planning may be limited.

- Absence of trust and openness between the owners of the business and non-owner-managers resulting in a reluctance to share future plans.

- There are costs associated with conducting strategic planning sessions, for smaller organizations it may be difficult to justify the costs.

- It may be difficult to link engagement in big companies type of strategic planning and the performance of an SME.

- SMEs focus on the short to medium terms, change courses often and quickly and may therefore not be able to see a strategic plan through. The quantity and frequency of changes may render the process academic.

What is necessary is for SMEs to adopt those aspects of strategic planning that assist their case as opposed to copying and pasting the practices of bigger companies. The strategic planning has to be flexible enough to enable a business to exploit opportunities as they present themselves. In view of the general weakness of systems and processes in SMEs, undertaking strategic planning can enforce a needed element of formalization and preservation of institutional memory as opposed to the strategy only existing in the head of the business owner. While this may not necessarily result in immediate performance advantages, as the business grows it lays the foundations for corporate discipline and strong corporate governance.

Main elements of strategic planning necessary for SMEs are:

- articulation of the business purpose;

- clear definition of the desired future position;
- clarity on the business' current situation – in all respects;
- identification of specific actions to move from current position to future position; and
- acting, measuring and acting.

6.3.1.1. Articulation of the Business Purpose

What is the company's reason for existence? This is what guides the company's owners, the Board or Advisors, management and employees. Governance structures that are put in place are guided by the need to fulfill the stated purpose. Accountability, fairness, and transparency are assessed in the context of the articulated purpose.

6.3.1.2. Clear Definition of the Desired Future Position

The desired future position is the business' vision or destination statement. It provides an indicator of what the business will look like when it achieves its stated purpose. In that regard, it provides a yardstick for checking progress towards that destination. The clearer the stated vision the more appropriate will be the governance mechanisms. Where an SME comes up with a vision that is a copy of some big organization this may translate to burdensome corporate governance mechanisms that may take an inordinate amount of time to administer at the expense of working on the business itself.

6.3.1.3. Clarity on the Business' Current Situation

Analysis of the business' current situation includes both internal and external factors. Internal analysis looks at the strengths and weaknesses while external analysis focuses on opportunities and threats. It therefore includes identification of risks – legal, technological, regulatory, social such as pressure groups on environmental issues, etc. Clarity on the business current situation helps in the identification of the type of Board and or Advisors needed by the business. It also facilitates the assessment of available resources, including human resources, in terms of their capacity to drive the business.

6.3.1.4. Identification of Specific Actions to Move from Current Position to Future Position

Identification of specific actions with measurable outcomes of how the business intends to move from its current position to the future position is another critical element. The more specific the desired actions are the easier it becomes to hold those responsible accountable. Owners of SMEs are known for being hands-on. While this is not bad in itself it compromises their ability to focus on other critical areas of the business such as exploring growth opportunities. Hands-on-ness is in most cases a result of an absence of identified specific actions that need to be taken. Actions therefore evolve as implementation proceeds. Although this may be good for flexibility, it makes it difficult to delegate and hold others accountable. Focusing on the business' short-term specific actions with due consideration for long-term possibilities makes it possible for the strategic plan to retain an element of flexibility, a necessary ingredient for SMEs.

6.3.1.5. Acting, Measuring and Acting

Working the plan is more important than the plan itself. Although documenting the plan is important, the documentation does not need to be perfect but needs to give the necessary guidance. To that effect governance mechanisms focus more on implementation of the plan than, as is the case in big organizations, the presentation of a perfect strategic plan document for approval by a Board and shareholders.

Figure 6.2: SME Strategic Planning.

Engaging in strategic planning and having a plan in place enables the entrepreneur to share their vision and strategic objectives. The process of sharing assists the owner/entrepreneur to think through their sometimes-unwritten plans and crystallize them. The objective is to achieve clarity in order to be able to track progress and not necessarily to have a big strategic plan document as tends to be the case in large organizations. Branson of Virgin indicates how from the time his businesses were SME to now the plan has been documented in a few words as he puts it, if it can't fit on the back of an envelope then it is too complicated (Figure 6.3).

To this day I don't make formal business plans, but am always crystal clear on the concept of the business. We have a saying at Virgin, if your pitch can't fit on the back of an envelope, then it's too complicated. In fact, we have written many business plans on the back of beer mats and envelopes – they have gone on to become successful companies like Virgin Australia.

Source: https://www.virgin.com/richard-branson/the-most-important-part-of-your-business-plan

---

Figure 6.3: Branson on Planning.

6.3.2. Structures

A major weakness in SME structures are high-levels of overlap between ownership and the board and between ownership and management because of the level of involvement of owners in the running of their businesses. While this may result in faster decision-making and the absence of the perennial agency-principal problems found in bigger organizations, it has its own problems. In the governance of the company a major problem is that of conflict of interest and separation of the business from the owner's personal life, interests, finances, assets and family among others. Further, that decision makers are also involved in the day-to-day running of the business may prevent them from having a broader view of the business resulting in over focusing on operational issues at the expense of more strategic issues. In bigger organizations corporate governance structures include the presence of non-executive directors and independent directors on the board. While for SMEs it may not be possible to have these, having at least one non-executive director or advisor is recommended. Where funds permit, the appointment of both non-executive and independent directors mitigates dysfunctional conflicts of interest and offers the following benefits:

- Board independence as a result of the balance of power within it;
- More objective decision-making that is guided by the interests of the organization;
- Appointment of the best candidates to the board in terms of relevant knowledge, skills, experience and capacity as opposed to being purely guided by ownership and relationships;
- Ensuring the transparent appointment of qualified key personnel in the management structures beyond family and or ownership;
- Installation of a framework for the delegation of authority, role clarity, and minimization of dysfunctional power struggles.

In situations where funds are limited, it remains critical for the SME to make board appointments formal and to clearly spell out the responsibilities and powers of those so appointed the objective being the avoidance of confusion and conflict during decision-making.

Some steps to be followed during the appointment process are:

- Thorough background checks to ensure that the people being appointed are both qualified and have integrity;
- Strong leadership skills, especially if the person is to take the position of chairman;
- For the chairman the role should be clearly spelt out and in particular its relationship with the CEO position.

Other structure issues that SMEs can derive from those of bigger organizations are: Board Committees, Audit Committee, Company Secretary, and Business Continuity Mechanisms.

6.3.2.1. Board Committees

In SMEs having board committees depends on the size of the organization. In bigger SMEs the board committee structures are similar to those in big companies while in smaller SMEs there may be in the form of ad hoc project teams that focus on specific issues as they arise. What is critical is for such teams to be guided by clear terms of reference.

6.3.2.2. Audit Committee

Just as is the case for big companies a SME also needs an Audit Committee that oversees the both internal and external audit in order to identify risks as they arise and to monitor their possible impact on the business; ensure integrity of financial reporting and ensure that reported information is accurate in order to create trust among various stakeholders. The size of SMEs makes it difficult to have an Audit Committee that is as good as that in big companies, this can be mitigated by ensuring that the committee is at least chaired by a noon-executive director. This is easier to implement in non-owner managed SMEs. In owner managed SMEs the Audit Committee function tends not to exist. The absence of an independent oversight on a company's financial and other reporting exposes SMEs to unidentified risks and also makes them less attractive to investors and hence hampering their ability to grow. SMEs as they grow could enhance their growth opportunities by putting systems in place to ensure an independent opinion on their operations. This can be achieved by soliciting the services of external auditors even if there is no legal requirement to do so.

6.3.2.3. Company Secretary

To function effectively the board needs a qualified and efficient company secretary. Ordinarily the responsibilities of a company secretary are:

- To provide directors both as a group and as individuals guidance on the duties, responsibilities and limits of power and authority;
- Staying abreast of any legal changes that affect the operations of the company and ensuring that the Board is updated of such developments;
- Minute taking during meetings, sending out agendas and Board papers for meetings and generally servicing the needs of the Board.

In some SMEs it may not be possible to have a company secretary this, however, does not mean that the function would be neglected as the duties can be allocated to another senior position. The outcomes expected from the functions are: ensuring the effective functioning of the Board and ensuring that the company complies with any applicable legislation and corporate governance.

Structures keep in check dysfunctional conflicts of interest, exposure to risks, threats to business continuity and ensure the efficient operations of the Board and compliance with legal requirements. Corporate governance structures should be viewed as more than a tick box exercise. Companies have been known to have corporate governance structures only for purposes of impressing external parties. Thus becomes apparent when the companies experience problems that clearly point to either the complete absence of an independent board or having a board only in word with owner-managers making all supposed to be board decisions.

6.3.3. Organization Structure

Organizational structure refers to the formal packing of jobs in an organization. It clarifies responsibilities and formal lines of reporting and of authority. Work is divided in a manner that clarifies responsibility boundaries and coordinates activities ensuring that resources are allocated with due consideration of the strategy. Good corporate governance requires that the organization's structures are guided by both the strategy and other subsidiary factors such as the size of the organization both in terms of employees and span of activities, level of use of technology and challenges and opportunities in the environment.

Six elements guide the development of an organization's structure, these are:

- Specialization of work;
- Departmentalization of similar or related jobs;
- Chain of command from the highest to the lowest position in the organization;
- Span of control;
- Level of centralization or decentralization; and
- Degree of formalization.

6.3.3.1. Specialization of Work

Specialization of work involves designing jobs clearly defining their responsibilities and limits. The extent to which work is specialized has a bearing on the nature of an organization's structure as it has implications on division of labor with each specializing in specific tasks. Although specialization is more prevalent in large organizations it is also found in SMEs or entrepreneurial firms. Specialization makes employees less flexible and therefore unable to work across different skills areas. While this makes for easier governance it is burdensome for SMEs where an employee has to work across different skills areas due to limited ability to recruit more people. Specialization offers the opportunity for employees to be experts in their areas, which could lead to improved productivity and reduced risks related to production errors. Its downside is that it can make-work monotonous, less challenging and less satisfying.

6.3.3.2. Departmentalization

Departmentalization involves grouping together similar or related jobs. Departmentalization can be based on functions, processes, products, geographical location, customers, specific assignment or a combination of these in the form of a matrix.

Functional: Functional departmentalization involves grouping activities according to the functions performed for example: production, marketing, sales, finance and human resources management. Through this approach the functions are headed by specialists in the specific fields. Although functional departmentalization promotes coordination, integration across departments and tight controls within the department, it tends to lead to centralization and a bureaucratic form of decision-making and an inability to change quickly when the need arises. Functional departmentalization is not that prevalent within SMEs because to start with there may not be enough managers to head-up the functions.

Customers: Customers based departmentalization groups activities according to the characteristics of the customers being served.

Products: This involves grouping activities according to the products or services produced or provided. All the resources together with authority are under the responsible manager. For example, a firm may produce two major lines of products such as: Cleaning products and edibles. Jobs are then grouped accordingly. Where the organization is big each grouping may represent a complete organization with layers of management. Such a structure facilitates product specialization by respective units. One of its disadvantages is that the various units may lose site of the objectives and values of the bigger organization. Separation also results in duplication of some positions which, from the perspective of the holding company makes it an expensive method of grouping jobs.

Processes: Jobs are grouped according to processes involved in providing a service or producing goods. This form of departmentalization is appropriate when specialized equipment or systems are used during a critical part of the production process.

Geography: This form involves grouping jobs according to the location of operations. This could be based on region, country or even town. It is largely found in international organizations where there is need to address specificities of for example a country or region. Although is increases focus on the customer's environment it can be expensive because of duplication of positions. For most SMEs financial constraints mitigate against this governance framework.

Taskforce based departmentalization: Jobs are grouped based on projects being implemented. This form is popular with project-oriented and based organizations. A project-based organization or firm is one where projects and programmes are taken as critical forms of organization for achieving strategic objectives coupled with needing specific human resources management practices to execute its mandate. Almost all the operations of such an organization are organized in the form of projects and whatever permanent structures exist their reason to be is to fulfill administrative functions.

The reason for project-based organizing is to escape the problems associated with bureaucratic organizing given that a project is task specific and time bound which makes it possible to exercise more control especially when dealing with complex assignments. The unit of control is the project and not the department as is the case in traditional bureaucratic organizations.

Matrix based departmentalization: The matrix combines different structures as necessitated by circumstances. It is therefore a hybrid approach to grouping jobs. For example, it can combine functional and task or project-based formats. In this setup an employee can report to multiple bosses so that there is no single line of command but multiple. Reporting structures run both horizontally and diagonally because of multiple reporting relationships. Although mostly used in project environments it is also found in non-project setups where employees may have a staff function relationship with managers in specific line functions while also maintaining their own reporting line with their own managers.

6.3.3.3. Chain of Command

Chain of command refers to the top-to-bottom reporting relationships among jobs. It clarifies formal lines of responsibility and authority.

6.3.3.4. Span of Control

Span of control refers to the limits placed on a job regarding the number of subordinates a supervisor may have or the areas for which a manager is responsible. Where work is routine a supervisor may have many subordinates but where it is complex the number of subordinates is less. The general guide is that the span of control should facilitate effective supervision leading to acceptable levels of productivity. A narrow span of control is associated with better supervision and subordinate-manager communication. It, however, results in a taller structure as layers of supervisors are likely to be more. A wider span of control results in less layers but the increased number of subordinates reduces chances of direct communication between the supervisor and subordinate. At the end of the day span of control is determined by: the competency levels of the supervisor and the supervised, the nature of the work being performed, methods of communication and the general management style. All these factors considered the Board has to ensure that spans of control for, in particular, executives will facilitate the attainment of organizational objectives. Budgetary constraints in growing SMEs tend to result in wide spans of control which end up compromising both efficiency and effectiveness.

6.3.3.5. Centralization or Decentralization

Centralization and decentralization refer to the distribution of decision-making power in an organization. Under a centralized system decisions are made by the most senior positions and the rest of the employees simply implement without question. In a decentralized system although the final decision is made by the most senior position there is a consultative purpose that enables almost all levels to take part. Further, employees are empowered to made decisions that concern their respective work areas. Centralization is ideal for organizations operating in a stable environment, skills levels among lower positions are significantly less than those in management because of the nature of work, the organization is operating in crisis mode, or where the organization is very large. Decentralization on the other hand is more suitable where: the environment is complex and turbulent, decisions that need to be made are significant and there are no differences in skills levels between managers and their subordinates, and the company's operations are spread out in different regions creating need for decisions to be made closest to the action.

6.3.3.6. Degree of Formalization

Formalization is about the extent to which work is structured in a manner that adheres to rigid procedures and channels of communication. Where the level of formalization is high there are clear job descriptions that guide the actions of every employee. People generally do not work across their job functions and there is limited sharing of work or working across teams. Every activity is guided by clearly spelt out rules, procedures and processes that have to be adhered to. Deviation from set rules attracts penalties. Where formalization is slow employees have high degrees of freedom in how they do their work and deviation from guiding rules does not necessarily attract penalties. Low formalization is usually associated with entrepreneurial organizations and or SMEs. While it has benefits therein also lies the source of poor corporate governance in SMEs. The high-levels of informalization left unchecked end up exposing a business to various risks whose origins can be traced back to weak guidelines, procedures rules among other things.

6.3.4. Types of Organization Structures

Organization structures can be classified into two broad types: mechanistic and organic.

6.3.4.1. Mechanistic Structure

A mechanistic structure has high-levels of specialization, departmentalization, and formalization, spans of control are narrow with a clear chain of command, and decisions are made by the most senior positions in the organization. Mechanistic structures are more suitable for mature companies operating in stable environments. Jobs are organized by function with each function representing a sub-organization and being represented in at a senior level. Determination of the functions is guided by the strategic plan. As illustrated in Figures 6.4, the structure can be organized based on regions, products and functions.

Figure 6.4: Examples of Functional structures.

This type of structure may not be ideal for entrepreneurial companies or SMEs as they are generally in a dynamic state.

6.3.4.2. Organic Structures

Characterized by teams that are cross-functional and cross-hierarchical, in an organic structure there is free flow of information in an environment with wide spans of control, low formalization with decentralized decision-making. It is suitable for organizations operating in unstable environments. This form of structure changes in line with business changes in size and focus as it progresses through its lifecycle. Organic designs of include Team structure, Matrix project structure and Boundary-less structures, which encompass Virtual, Network and Modular organizations.

Matrix model is perhaps the most common organic structure. It has reporting structures that run both horizontally and diagonally because of multiple reporting points for employees. The structure facilitates sharing of expertize making it efficient as each expert resource is fully utilized, a desired situation in an SME.

6.3.5. Organization Chart

An organization chart makes visible an organization's structure as it illustrates the formal reporting lines by job title. It is clear on compartmentalization of work, chain of command, span of control, unity of command and authority. Main forms of organizational charts are: vertical, horizontal or circular (Figures 6.5–6.7).

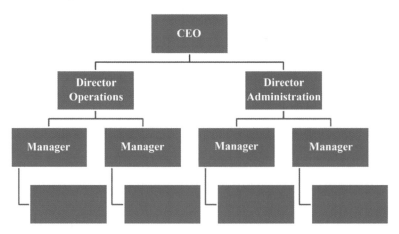

Figure 6.5: Vertical Chart.

Figure 6.6: Horizontal Chart.

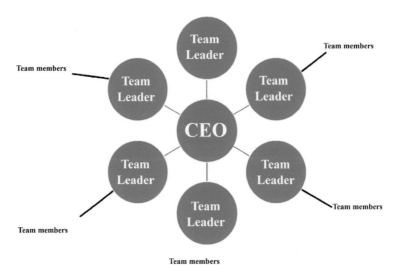

Figure 6.7: Circular organization chart.

Linked to the structure on its own does not provide sufficient guidance, as it does not detail the specific responsibilities of each job hence the need for job profiles and specifications. If the structure clarifies governance issues at the level of the shareholder, the board and the CEO, job profiles and specifications provide governance guidelines at the level of individual employees as illustrated in Figure 6.8.

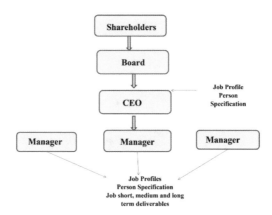

Figure 6.8: Place of Job profiles in corporate governance.

6.3.6. Job Description and a Job Specification

A job description is a critical component of organizational governance as it clarifies the contractual obligations of the employee to the employer. It is through it that an employee is held accountable for their performance. It clearly articulates identification of the job in terms of its title and which position it reports to, the reason for its existence, responsibilities and duties, what authority it has, the positions it supervises, resources under its control and risks associated with the job. In the corporate governance of an SME key jobs for which there has to be clarity include: Managing Director or CEO, Head of Finance, Head of Marketing, Head of Production.

CEO Job Description

Job Title: Chief Executive Officer

Reports to: Board through the Board Chairman

Directly supervises: Finance Manager; Production Manager; Marketing Manager and Human Resources Manager.

Executive Limitations: The executive limitations of the position are as stated in the Board of Directors Policies document.

Areas of responsibility:

-       Directing firm operations in a manner consistent with the vision presented by the Board;

-       Implementing the strategic plan agreed on with the Board;

-       Developing operational strategies aligned to the main strategic objectives;

-       Building the firm's capacity to achieve its objectives;

-       Preparing and submitting budgets in line with agreed plans;

-       Ensuring company compliance with the legal framework and industry standards;

-       Ensuring quality control in al operational sites.

Specific deliverables: Deliverables for any specific period shall be as detailed in the annual performance contract.

Figure 6.9: Example of CEO Job Description.

6.4. MANAGING CHANGE

Strategy implementation goes hand in hand with change making organization change a critical part of an organization's strategy. Change can occur in several areas of an organization for example it could be in the: vision, mission, strategic objectives, structure, culture, systems, management and leadership, and technology.

Organizational change may affect processes, strategies, management, and day-to-day operations in all in a bid to either maximize performance or to service. It is part and parcel of the process of strategy implementation. Some changes are planned and others are not. What falls in the realm of corporate governance is that change which is planned and therefore proactive. There are instances though when change is unplanned as a result of the organization reacting to unforeseen circumstances. This type of change tends to test an organization's corporate governance mechanisms as decisions need to be made fast and in most cases with limited guidelines.

Studies have emphasized that to stay ahead of the competition organizations need to be more cost-effective and efficient manner, and that demands continuously changing (Benn et al., 2014). Change can be hard (affecting technical issues) or soft (affecting people issues) but in both cases needs to be managed from the highest level in the organization. This is particularly true in the case of SMEs where systems are still in their formative stages making it critical that as the organization is continually renewing its direction, structures, and capabilities, the process is managed to ensure that whatever changes are taking place they are aligned to the strategic objectives.

6.4.1. Nature of organizational change

Van de Ven and Poole (1995) posits that organizational change can be explained by dialectic theory, lifecycle theory and teleological theory of management. Dialectical theory views the organization as a multi-cultural society made up of diverse values. When a point is reached where one set of values dominates over others the organization adopts them and change occurs. According to this view it is necessary to establish common organizational goals and values that produce desired changes. Lifecycle theory proposes that the organization is an entity that, as a result of external environment influence, goes through a lifecycle whose stages are birth, maturation, growth, and decline. Changes taking place in the organization are a reflection of the stage it is at in its lifecycle. From a governance perspective those mechanisms put in place are consistent with the stage the organization is at in its lifecycle. Teleological theory states that an organization envisions a desired future state and through a continuous process of goal setting, execution, evaluation, restructuring and back to goal setting it makes necessary changes in order to achieve the ideal state (Vakola et al., 2013).

Organizational change can be categorized as evolutionary or revolutionary and the level of board involvement may be influenced by the category of the change. Evolutionary change can be in the form of what Handy (1989) described as strategic drift while revolutionary change could be in the form of transformational change. Change classification is generally guided by the speed of the change as shown in Table 6.2.

Table 6.2: Types and Characteristics of Change

Type of Change	Characteristics
Discontinuous	Rapid shifts in either strategy, structure or culture, or in all three; single, abrupt shift from the past; triggered by major internal problems or by considerable external shock
Incremental	Individual parts of an organization separately deal with one problem and one objective at a time; change implemented through successive, limited, and negotiated shifts
Smooth incremental	Evolves slowly in a systematic and predictable way at a constant rate
Bumpy incremental Punctuated equilibrium	Periods of relative peace punctuated by acceleration in the pace of change
Continuous	Ability to change continuously in a fundamental manner to keep up with the fast-moving pace of change – organization-wide strategies
Bumpy Continuous	Relative peace punctuated by acceleration in the pace of change in the case for organization-wide strategies.

Source: Adapted from Todnem By (2005).

6.4.2. Dealing with Planned Change

Planned change in organizations is driven by:

- Change in strategic thrust;
- Changes in operating environment both inside and outside the organization;
- Planned technological changes;
- Executive ego.

6.4.2.1. Change in Strategic Thrust

An organization may make a deliberate decision to change its strategic thrust for example in terms of primary markets, the product, methods of delivery and service resulting in the need to reconfigure various processes to bring them in line with the new organizational priorities.

6.4.2.2. Changes in Operating Environment Both Inside and Outside the Organization

The operating environment may change in terms of for example the legal framework, societal expectations, economy, technological changes, demands from environmental pressure groups and political pressures. Within the organization changes may be a result of relations with employees, financial constraints and a culture that is no longer supportive of organizational objectives.

6.4.2.3. Executive Ego

Some planned organizational changes have nothing to do with the organization itself but everything to do with the chief executive's ego. For example, they may want certain products or services introduced in order to look better than competition even if there is no business case for the changes. It is such changes that the board needs to be alert to as they could have negative repercussions for the organization.

6.4.3. Change Management Theories

Lewin's 3-Stage and Force Field Model, Cummings and Huse (1989) and Lippit, Watson and Wesley model theories are common theories of planned change which organizations use to ground their change processes. Change processes have failed partly as a result of organizational failure to handle the process in a clear and appropriate framework or failure by the board and management to elicit the assistance of professionals.

6.4.3.1. Lewin's 3-Stage Model of Change

According to Kurt Lewin's model for change to be successful it has to go through three stages:

- unfreezing the current situation;
- moving to the new situation; and
- refreezing the new situation.

During the unfreezing stage areas to be changed are identified together with possible challenges and enablers. This stage may involve changing the CEO or the whole executive team or reorganization of departments and or divisions. Such an action could be a result of identifying forces for the change and forces against the change. Where it is identified that the current crop of management may be a hindrance to the change, the board could decide to eliminate the points of resistance through separation. The three-stage model is used closely with Lewin's force field analysis (Figure 6.9). According to force field analysis in any change situation there are forces in favor and forces against the change. The challenge is to strengthen forces for the change while weakening or eliminating those against the change. The forces may be at a macro, micro and individual level. Macro forces are usually outside the organization.

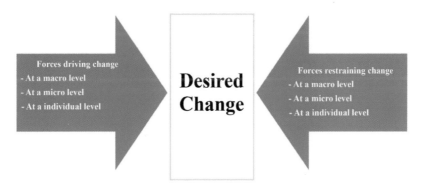

Figure 6.10: Kurt Lewin Force Field Analysis.

Moving to the new situation may involve several initiatives largely by management with the board playing an oversight role to ensure alignment with the intended objectives of the change initiative. The new situation may for example entail change structures, processes and procedures.

The refreezing stage involves building supportive structures for the change such as a performance management system whose measures ensure that the change is embedded into the organization. Although the board may not be involved in the day-to-day operations it remains responsible for the successful execution of the change and in particular for ensuring that the changes do not expose the organization to unnecessary risks.

6.4.3.2. Cummings and Huse Model

Cummings and Huse (1989) model view change as a cyclical process involving eight major steps:

- Identification of a problem;
- Soliciting the services of an expert or experts to conduct a deeper analysis of the problem;
- Data collection and analysis of the exact elements that need to be

changed;
- Giving feedback to the organization;
- Joint problem diagnoses and identification of further areas that need additional data;
- Joint action planning;
- Implementation of the changes; and
- Post-implementation data gathering and assessment.

6.4.3.3. Lippit, Watson and Wesley – Seven Phases of Change

Seven phases of change model focuses on the role of the change agent and has the following seven steps:
- Problem diagnosis;
- Assessment of the motivation for change and the capacity to implement it;
- Assessment of the resources and motivation of the change agent which includes their commitment and capacity to see the process through;
- Defining progressive stages of change;
- Clearly articulating the roles and responsibilities allocated to change agents;
- Maintenance of the change through continuous communication, feedback, and coordination of the group;
- Timed removal of the change agent when change has been institutionalized.

Planned approaches to change have been criticized for failing to note that much change-taking place, especially in SMEs is not planned but rather a response to rapidly changing environments. Where a plan does exist it is often disrupted by developments in the environment. This is one area where SME owners disagree or find themselves in conflict with boards that would be wanting things done in a more planned and orderly manner. The planned approach has therefore been criticized as:
- Biased in favor of small incremental change and not for major organization-wide changes where there is need for rapid transformation (Burnes, 2004);
- Assuming that organizations exist in a stable environment where change can be implemented in a step by step linear manner

(Bamford and Forrester, 2003);

- Incapable of handling a crisis where decisions have to be taken fast using incomplete information (Burnes, 2004);
- Assumes that all the major stakeholders of the change process are supportive and therefore ignores the politics factor in any change process;
- Not suitable for instances where the risk of failure is high.

6.4.4. Classifications of Change

Where corporate governance is concerned it is critical to understand the nature of the change taking place to ensure that the organization does not end up with unintended results. Having identified change as planned or emergent, within these domains change can also be classified as evolutionary, revolutionary or transformational with each dictating different approaches to change management and therefore having different implications for corporate governance.

6.4.5. Evolutionary Change

Evolutionary change aims at continuous improvement. It therefore tends to be intermittent, gradual and narrowly focused. It is what was described by Handy (1989) as strategic drift which is a gradual change that unfolds in a subtly manner to an extent that it is not noticeable until it is too late to do anything about it. Such change can be both negative and positive. It becomes negative when it is not directed and is happening almost unconsciously as the organization has no way of extracting benefits from it. The board may not even be aware of this type of change as it tends to take place at the lower levels of the organization. Its subtle nature, however, makes it potentially dangerous as it is the kind of change which can find its way into slowly changing organizational processes, procedure and practices and making them part of the organizational culture.

6.4.6. Revolutionary Change

Revolutionary change is broadly focused, dramatic and rapid. It usually occurs when the organization is trying to keep pace with developments in the environment for example, when the organization's method of delivering customer value fails to fulfill demands making it necessary to completely overhaul the processes. Because of the speed with which such change is implemented it may expose the organization to risks as a result of adoption of ill considered decisions.

Due to the increasing pace of globalization of almost every organization, fast technological innovation, major shifts in social and demographic trends, emergence of virtual organizations, deregulation and regulation all organizations whether large or SME are subject to revolutionary change. This has made the management of organizational change more complicated than that witnessed under evolutionary change. While large organizations with fully developed processes and systems may be well positioned to handle such changes, for SMEs they can result in complete annihilation of the organization. Three forms of revolutionary change affect SMEs: innovation, reengineering and restructuring (Burke, 2013).

6.4.6.1. Innovation

Innovation involves the successful use of resources and skills that are specifically required in the creation of new goods, technologies, and services in a novel way. The actions lead to a major positive transformation of the organization and or its product offering giving it competitive advantage. In that regard, there are governance issues relating to innovation (Deschamps, 2013; Deschamps and Nelson, 2014). Innovation governance is defined by Deschamps (2013) as mechanisms that are used "to align goals, allocate resources and assign decision-making authority for innovation, across the company and with external parties." The mechanisms include:

- Clearly articulating who will play what role in the process;
- Clarifying levels of decision-making;
- Clearly stating commitments and responsibilities of the main actors;
- Spelling out the underlying values of the innovation initiatives;
- Specifying how the success of the innovation will be measured and tracked;
- Deciding on budgetary limits and acceptable variances;
- Prioritising activities across units in a manner aligned to the strategic intent;
- Establishing communication and decision-making protocols.

Deschamps (2013) identifies five innovation governance responsibilities of the board which are:

- Auditing the effectiveness of the innovation;
- Strategy review to ensure continued alignment;
- Performance review to ensure that critical targets are being met;
- Risk management to ensure that the organization is not being exposed to unnecessary risk; and
- CEO and top management nomination to ensure a continuous pool of needed expertize.

6.4.6.2. Reengineering

This involves radically redesigning a process and the fundamental principles guiding it in order to have a significant impact on performance measures such as quality, cost, service and turnaround speed.

6.4.6.3. Restructuring

It occurs when an organization experiences a rapid decline in performance (Nica, 2013) necessitating the need for managers to turn the things around through restructuring in order to return the organization to acceptable levels of performance. This can be achieved through for example simplification of the organizational structure by eliminating some levels to make it flatter and more cost-effective, reducing the general number of employees to match productivity levels, and letting go of non-performing units. It is a responsibility of the board as part of its oversight role. Good governance requires that the board takes a leading role in such an exercise as management tends to be conflicted.

The role of the board in revolutionary change is better understood from the perspective of McKinsey 7s Model that emphasizes the importance of alignment among the hard (strategy, structure, systems) and soft (shared values, skills, staff, style) components of an organization.

McKinsey 7s Model views organizational change as a system wide phenomenon that answers questions that arise from strategy implementation. The framework facilitates systematic and comprehensive analysis of a change situation through addressing specific questions relating to seven areas: strategy, structure and systems on the one hand and skills, staff, management and leadership style, and shared values and therefore lends itself for use in the governance of organizational change. According to the model, the success of change depends on the extent to which there is alignment in the seven areas.

Table 6.3: Governance Key Questions That Arise from the 7s Model

7s Component	Key Questions
Strategy	What business are we in? What business should we be in? What are our chances of winning? What is going to be our winning formula? Our strategic objectives? What environmental factors are going to affect our intentions?
Structure	Is our current structure appropriate? If not how should we be organized? How can we make our structure facilitate faster decision-making?
Systems	What are the main systems that drive the business? Are they adequate? Do we need new systems?
Skills	Do we have the critical skills we need in the short, medium and long-term? What should we do to get or keep them?
Staff	Do we have sufficient quantities of the required skills? Do we need to recruit? Do we have redundant skills that must be eliminated?
Style	Does our leadership and management style support our goals? Which parts of our style are likely to impede progress; Are we able to change the style through encouraging individuals to change or should we replace people?
Shared values	What are the values we all hold dear? Are they shared across the organization? Are they consistent with our chosen strategy? Which values need to be changed?

6.4.6.4. Transformational Change

Transformational change is organization-wide, sudden and radical and is usually a result of shocks coming from outside the organization. It is solely driven from the top by the board and is not negotiable. Such change shifts the organization in a completely different trajectory. The change is fast and usually results in a complete change of the CEO and executive team.

6.4.7. Leadership and Management Style

Regardless of the form of change taking place in an organization, there is a governance role for the board in ensuring that the leadership and management style in the organization do not impede the desired change. Different styles of leadership are associated with different forms of change. The board has to ensure that the leadership in place has the capacity to drive the desired change. Concerning leadership role Kotter (1999) notes the importance of creating an inspiring vision for organizational change and appropriately communicating the same to employees.

It has been established that the nature and style of leadership are major determinants of successful implementation of change with some styles being associated with change more than others (Anderson, 2013). Participative leadership and transformational leadership have been associated with reduced resistance to change by employees. Further, leaders who maintain a positive relationship with their subordinates face less resistance to change initiatives. It is the board that has to ensure that the subsisting type of leadership is appropriate. Further, it has to ensure that organizational politics, which has been known to impede change, is dealt with.

Because organizations are a mixture of different interest groups, within the board, the management team and between the management team and employees turf wars are always there. When changed is introduced it can be resisted by some groupings in the organization for no reason other than being against the person or group that would have initiated the change. This is more likely in organizations with a weak and or conflicted board. As part of corporate governance a board is accountable for failed desired change in an organization.

6.5. ACCOUNTABILITY

As a key component of CG, accountability refers to all the internal parties being answerable for their actions both within and outside the company. Where the Board is concerned accountability is enforced through the assessment of Board effectiveness and also during shareholders' meetings. Management is usually assessed through performance reviews. Such assessments are easier in non-owner managed businesses. In owner managed businesses where there is no separation between ownership and management it is more difficult to conduct performance and effectiveness assessments. In non-owner managed companies accountability is partly enforced through consequences management, such enforcement is difficult to implement in owner or family managed businesses.

Although it may not be practical for an SME to use the same accountability mechanisms as those in big organizations, it is good corporate governance practice for the owner-managers to subject themselves to some form of candid self-assessment and to also invite honest third party assessments.

Honest assessments can result in training and development of directors and management to make them more effective.

Board and management accountability stretches to accountability to other stakeholders outside the organization. Affected areas include legal and regulatory compliance, adherence to rules, codes and industry standards. Failure to comply can expose to risks such as substantial fines, criminal liability, damage to brand reputation and being shunned by both clients and suppliers.

In owner-managed businesses where there is no Board, the owner is responsible for ensuring all forms of compliance. In the line of doing business not all owner-managers pay adequate attention to compliance issues. Such businesses have to develop governance mechanisms to address accountability issues that relate to compliance. Where the SME has a Board, the latter is ultimately accountable for compliance although management is the one responsible for implementation. Whether administered through the owner manager or the Board, the key issues are:

- Ensuring that the company complies with relevant legislation;
- Adherence to non-binding industry regulations, codes and standards;
- Appreciation of the effect of non-compliance with relevant laws, regulations, codes and standards on the company;
- Making risks associated with compliance integral to the internal risk management mechanisms;
- Institute effective risk management mechanisms.

6.5.1. Company Compliance with Relevant Legislation

Some of the legislation includes:

- Tax laws
- Employment laws
- Company registration returns

6.5.1.1. Adherence to non-binding industry regulations, codes and standards

These vary from industry to industry, may be non-binding but non-adherence tends to result in some form of censure.

6.5.1.2. Appreciation of the effect of non-compliance

The monetary implications of non-compliance need to be calculated so that they are known and are subjected to a cost benefit analysis. Although the intention may be to comply, this is not always possible. This is especially true for businesses operating in developing economies where there may be contradictions in regulations. In such situations the intention to comply is overshadowed by the gains of non-compliance which may far outweigh those of compliance. For example, laws and regulations that clearly stand in the way of business to an extent that the business may go under if they are followed or that are not supportive of the business model run the risk of being ignored or violated by entrepreneurs.

6.5.1.3. Managing risks

Risk management in SMEs tends to focus on being reactive and absorbing risks though creating redundancies and rarely includes proactive measures. SMEs have poor management for example of risks associated with failing to comply yet some have been forced to go out of business or to suffer major unplanned for losses due to such risks.

The risks and organization could face have to be identified and everything done to mitigate their possible negative impact. In owner managed companies the owner or some designated senior persons must be satisfied that possible organizational risks are identified, monitored and controlled.

Some risks faced by SMEs whose potential impact is often underestimated are:

- Human Resources risks;
- Business or market risks;
- Plant and property risks;
- Information technology risks;
- Risks associated with operational liability;
- Production interruption risks;
- Transportation risks;
- Environmental risks.

6.5.1.4. Human Resources Risks

Human resources risks include: loss of key personnel through resignation, illness, accident or death; mass job action; en-mass resignations and setting up in competition and incapacitation of the entrepreneur/owner. All the eventualities could result in loss of work input, failure to service clients and poor financial performance and even demise. HR risk management involves all critical business areas. One of the main ways of managing HR risk is ensuring that the organization has a self replenishing pipeline of skilled employees for its critical positions. This can be achieved through strategic talent management. SME usually work with limited budgets for employee training and development. Under such circumstances it becomes critical to clearly identify key positions, key skills and competences required in those positions and people who hold those skills or those who can be developed to acquire those skills. Talent management can be defined as inclusive or exclusive. Where bigger and better resourced organizations may have the luxury of classifying all employees as talent of key and spending indiscriminately on their training and development, in SMEs a more exclusive definition leads to a more focused approach. An inclusive definition could therefore put the organization at risks as budgetary constraints may lead to half-baked employees who fail to deliver the desired results.

6.5.1.5. Business or Market Risks

Included among business or market risks are:

- Decrease in the demand for the product due to unforeseen developments;
- Customers' inability to pay on time both of which could lead to serious cash flow problems
- and failure to meet customer demand due to inadequate production capacity resulting in customers changing suppliers.

In the absence of governance mechanisms an organization may have a high internal focus and be unable or not have the mechanisms for keeping track of developments in the market and end up either over supplying what is no longer needed or failing to supply what is needed.

6.5.1.6. Plant and Property Risks

Plant and property risks include damage though fire, floods and other natural disasters; damage due to employee actions intended or unintended; machine breakdowns and normal plant wear and tear. SMEs tend to overlook the need to adequately insure plant and equipment and depend on hoping for the best. When disaster strikes there is interruption in production and failure to satisfy market needs and to meet financial targets. In worst-case scenarios it results in business closure.

6.5.1.7. Information Technology Risks

Although information technology has assisted many SMEs to leapfrog bigger players it comes with associated risks some of which are: damage to the company's computer hard drive, truant employees selling a company's client database or other strategic data to competition; leakage of company classifies information resulting in loss of reputation. Another side of this form of risk is where an SME holds on to old technology that compromises its ability to deliver services to the satisfaction of clients. Poor ICT systems in SMEs lead to customers losing faith in the business' capacity to deliver.

6.5.1.8. Risks Associated with Operational Liability

Operational liability risks include employees making mistakes that have a negative effect on the product and or customer resulting in the company having to pay for damages or loss of business by a third party. Corporate governance mechanisms facilitate the identification of such risks and formulating plans to address them. Operational risks that face SMEs include failures on the part of their suppliers leading to failure by the SME to fulfill orders. Although identification of the risks does not in itself eliminate the risks, it at least makes it possible to put in place alternative plans.

6.5.1.9. Production Interruption Risks

Other than disruptions related to the state of plant and equipment, production can also be interrupted by other factors such as employee strike action; weather conditions; major power cuts; non-availability of capital for raw materials; hold up of inputs beyond the control of the company; and failure to deliver by a sub-contractor.

6.5.1.10. Product Failure Risks

This occurs when the company's product fails to perform in the intended manner resulting to damages or losses being incurred by the client and the company paying a penalty which could be significant. This can also include product damage during transportation.

6.5.1.11. Environmental Risks

Environmental risk may arise where for example a company's products or inputs cause damage to the environment resulting in loss of reputation and liability for damages. This is a major risk for many companies in sectors such as mining and related industries.

The board or its equivalent should:

- Establish acceptable levels of risk tolerance;
- Establish a committee responsible for risk monitoring and management;
- Ensure that there is continuous risk assessment to avoid surprises;
- Establish understood frameworks and methodologies for dictating risks;
- Ensure that appropriate risk responses are taken;
- Regularly assess the effectiveness of the risk management mechanisms and reporting structures.
- Take corrective action when the need arises (see Figure 6.11).

Why Boards Must Step Up To Deter Corporate Scandals

Len Sherman Contributor ⓘ
I write about management priorities for long-term growth.

This month brought more fallout from the Wells Fargo consumer banking fraud, as the company fired three regional managers in its continuing efforts to deal with lawsuits from former workers, customers and investors, and ongoing investigations from the Department of Justice and other regulatory agencies.

Wells Fargo also recently stripped CEO Tim Sloan and seven of his top lieutenants of their 2016 bonuses, fired four other executives, and discontinued the stringent sales quotas that unwittingly incentivized bank employees to set up two million unauthorized consumer bank accounts. All of this comes as Wells Fargo braces for the release of findings from an independent board investigation, which is expected prior to what could be a contentious annual meeting with shareholders on April 25.

Multiple reports of illegal employee behaviors began flowing in to Wells Fargo's internal ethics hotline as early as 2005. "Everyone knew there was fraud going on," said a former branch manager who was fired after contacting both HR and the bank's ethics hotline about illegal accounts he had seen being opened. In 2013, the Los Angeles Times published a story about 30 Wells Fargo employees that were fired for opening unauthorized consumer bank accounts. Despite numerous subsequent internal and external reviews of its retail banking practices, Wells Fargo's incremental corrective actions were insufficient to stem ongoing fraudulent activity.

Figure 6.11: Risk of corporate scandals, Source: Adapted from https://www. forbes.com/sites/lensherman/2017/03/13/why-boards-must-step-up-to-deter-corporate-scandals/#2d01a00c1b79.

6.5.2. SMEs and Risk Management

Management of risks is one of the areas that underline the importance of an SME having a Board or external advisors as, being more focused on the external environment as opposed to the day-to-day operations of the business, they are better placed to objectively identify and assess risks. Risk management related failures are indicative of corporate governance failures as they point to a Board or its equivalent that has failed in one of its major responsibilities. Table 6.4 gives a list of some the explanations for risk management failure and Table 6.5 lists some failures that have been experienced and their causes. Although the examples given are form big organizations with Boards of Directors that ordinarily would have been expected to curb the risky activities, they amply illustrate the criticality of risk management and the need to balance the drive for profit with other the possibility of undesired outcomes. While big organizations may have the capacity to pay ensuing penalties, for SMEs this could spell the end of the company.

Table 6.4: Explanations for Failure in Risk Management

Reason for Failure
1. Board that lack expertize in enterprise risk management
2. Gaps in risk related governance at Board or management level or both
3. The Board not acting on risk issues even when reported – either out of ignorance or collusion or negligence
4. Weak internal audit, or absence of internal audit or ignoring advice from internal audit or internal audit that has no direct link to the Board
5. Weak internal controls that continue unchecked or that can be overridden by management without Board approval
6. Absence of thresholds for risk appetite
7. Defective risk culture that discourages whistle blowing
8. Risk management not factored into the strategies and the performance management system
9. Pay system that is not adjusted for risk
10. Failure to anticipate risk or to appreciate its possible impact

Some examples of Risk Management Failures are listed in Table 6.5.

Table 6.5: Examples of Risk Management Failures

Company	**Incident**	**Explanation**
Knight Capital	Software failure resulting in immediate pre-tax loss of USD440 million; over 50% loss in share price within two days	Pushed technology and neglected risk management
Volkswagen	Evading environmental compliance resulting in over 30 federal lawsuits and a reduction of 40% in share price	Enterprise wide risk assessments not conducted

General Motors	Recall of about 30 million cars recalled, law suits and forfeited USD900 million to US Gov,	Faulty ignition key
JP Morgan	London Whale trading scandal resulted in USD920 million in penalties, and USD6.2 billion in losses among other related penalties	Fixing risk controls was not prioritized by the bank. Profit motive was paramount (see Figure 6.11)

#BUSINESS NEWS JUNE 19, 2017 / 10:53 PM / 3 MONTHS AGO

Former JPMorgan trader Iksil links CEO Dimon to 'London Whale' losses

Reuters Staff

(Reuters) - Bruno Iksil, the former JPMorgan Chase & Co (JPM.N) trader at the center of the "London Whale" trading scandal, has accused the Wall Street bank's Chief Executive James Dimon of laying the ground for the $6.2 billion loss.

In an account on his website, Iksil, a French national who traded credit derivatives for JPMorgan in London, also blamed senior executives at the bank. (bit.ly/2sjf2WS)

"The senior executives chose Iksil to work as a screen for them in late 2010", he said.

The Chief Investment Office (CIO), where Iksil worked, lost $6.2 billion in trading in 2012, hurting the bank's reputation.

"When the CIO of JPMorgan had lost $1 billion dollar, JPMorgan as a whole had made $4 billion for itself net of its CIO loss," Iksil alleged.

"The JPMorgan CIO lost in whole $6.3 billion which led to an ultimate profit at JPMorgan of more than $25 billion in 2012," he said on the website.

The bank had to pay more than $1 billion and admit to wrongdoing to settle U.S. and British probes into the losses.

JPMorgan declined to comment.

Reporting by Arunima Banerjee in Bengaluru; Editing by Sriraj Kalluvila

Figure 6.12: Executive accountability compromised.

6.6. ENTREPRENEURS AND COMPLIANCE

Although the need for compliance is highlighted it is critical to understand the relationship between entrepreneurial firms or entrepreneurs and compliance legal frameworks, industry standards and other regulations affecting their businesses which at times create a culture of not being accountable.

6.6.1. Perceptions of Procedural Fairness

When SMEs perceive that there is procedural fairness experienced by small business in application of regulations they are more likely to comply. Perceptions SMEs have of, for example, tax authorities' influences their willingness to comply.

6.6.2. Regulatory Responsiveness to Entrepreneur Needs/ Challenges

When regulators are perceived as non-responsive or unreasonable, entrepreneurs opt to conduct some of their activities in the informal or shadow economy. That this not consistent with good corporate governance does not deter them even in instances where corporate governance structures seem to exist. Entrepreneurs tend to turn to what makes business sense for them as opposed to what is acceptable to the regulator. Examples where benefits are seen to exist in the shadow economy are escaping:

- Income and labor taxation;
- Burdensome and unsuitable regulations that increase a company's overheads;
- Government institutions corruption;
- Risks associated with currency instability;
- Risks associated with hyper inflation.

6.7. BUSINESS CONTINUITY – SUCCESSION PLANNING

One of the critical structures to be put in place in an SME is the succession plan as its absence is a major risk to business continuity. In the absence of a Board or in the presence of a weak Board owner-managers usually fail to plan for business continuity beyond their own tenure or to plan for the conversion of the business from owner or family control to a publicly listed entity or a non-listed entity run by management and an independent Board.

Another succession failure relates to mechanisms for handing the business over to the younger generation within the family.

Succession planning includes putting in place contingency measures for filling critical positions as and when they fall vacant given the generally low levels of critical skills within SMEs.

6.7.1. Succession Planning

Succession planning is part of business continuity planning as it adds depth to the organization's talent pool by ensuring that there is a pipeline of future technical and leadership expertize. Further, it ensures that positions with the highest impact are occupied by high performing incumbents. It is therefore first the responsibility of the board and secondly of the CEO. The process involves: identifying critical positions; conducting an analysis of the position and developing a succession plan for the position which may include interventions such as employee development, monitoring and evaluation (see Figure 6.12).

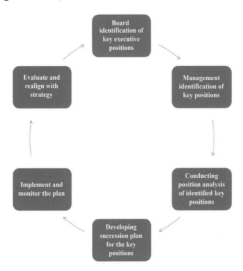

Figure 6.13: Succession Planning.

6.7.1.1. Identifying Critical Positions

Critical positions are identified by analyzing why a position is considered critical, its role in the attainment of strategic goals, the technical and specialized skills required for optimum performance. Considered at this stage is also whether the position is only filled by one person or several. Single person positions expose the organization to higher risk in the event of the person leaving hence the importance of identifying them and having a plan for ensuring continuity.

6.7.1.2. Conducting a Position Analysis

The stage of position analysis involves consideration of internal and external factors affecting the position. Questions that are addressed include:

- probability of the current incumbent leaving the organization;
- availability of possible internal replacements;
- availability of the skills in the labor market;
- price of skills on the labor market within context of company's ability to pay;
- Risks of an external hire becoming a wrong fit.

6.7.1.3. Developing a Succession Plan for the Position

The planning needs to be systematic and this is aided by using tried tools such as a succession planning grid that clearly identifies leadership potential and current and past performance. The process facilitates filtering out employees who are technically competent, perform well but have no leadership potential. The output of succession planning is a clear indication of employees in the talent pipeline that are ready for promotion and those that need further development.

6.7.1.4. Monitoring, Evaluation and Revision

Once developed the succession plan is implemented and this process includes monitoring, evaluation and revision on an ongoing basis. Monitoring and evaluation are conducted within the context of a transparent and well-understood performance management process that facilitates employee development.

6.7.2. CEO Succession

The position whose succession planning is most critical for corporate governance is that of CEO. Organizational success is to a large extent dependent on leadership performance. Continuity at the apex of the organization is therefore paramount and that responsibility rests with the

Board. According to Delloite (2013) activities relating to CEO succession must be continuous to ensure that risks are alleviated, possible successors are placed under on-going assessment in line with developments within the organization and in the environment, the board has ample opportunities to interact with possible successors and that the transition to the next CEO is smooth.

A perennial question regarding CEO succession is whether to make an internal or an external appointment. Each of the options presents advantages and disadvantages that need to be weighed as illustrated in the CEO succession experiences of Hewlett-Packard and Apple Inc. (Figure 6.13).

CEO Succession: From Within or from Without?

The appointment of Meg Whitman as CEO of Hewlett-Packard in 2011 marked the fourth time in six years that the technology company utilized an external successor to fill the position. Whitman's predecessor, Leo Apotheker (formerly of SAP), stepped down after less than 11 months on the job. Reports following Apotheker's resignation cited a major decline in stock price, poor sales forecasts, and a series of poorly executed strategic initiatives. Prior to Apotheker, CEO Mark Hurd had stepped down after allegations of unseemly behavior.

In 2011, Timothy Cook replaced the legendary Steve Jobs as CEO of Apple Inc. after having been with the company for 13 years. Prior to Jobs's resignation, Cook had served as COO for five years, and had temporarily taken over Jobs's role on three occasions during Jobs's medical leaves. Apple's board reported having "complete confidence that Tim [was] the right person to be [Apple's] next CEO." In the time since Cook took the reins, Apple's market value has increased by roughly $140 billion.

Source: Adapted from Aon Hewitt (2012, p.1)

Figure 6.14: CEO Succession – Hewlett – Packard and Apple Inc.

Key questions to be addressed by the board regarding CEO Succession include:

- Is the board driving the CEO succession process?
- Is CEO succession a routine topic discussed by the Board?
- Does the Board have regular face-to-face interactions with possible CEO successors?
- Does the Board have a plan?
- Is the plan private or confidential?

The board can improve its succession planning initiatives by:

- Outlining the future operating and leadership skills required for each position and benchmarking executives against the identified skills.
- Cast a wide net at recruitment stage in order to address the needs of constantly evolving organizations.
- Treat succession as a continuous process where management and the board keep abreast of unexpected transitions throughout the organization.

- Assign specific board committee or members to be responsible and accountable for the succession planning.
- Seek external strategic assistance in order to benchmark with industry practices.

6.8. SUMMARY AND CONCLUSION

This chapter highlighted that CG in SMEs is grounded in ethical and effective leadership that is responsible, accountable, fair and transparent. The chapter discusses leadership ethics and integrity and their relationship with corporate governance. Deontology and utilitarianism ethics theories were identified as assisting in understanding the actions of entrepreneurs. Controversies relating to ethical decision-making and who defines what is ethical and what is not were covered. Notwithstanding the controversies it was noted that being responsible and accountable were key issues in SME corporate governance. Being responsible was portrayed as including ensuring that the organization has a strategy and supportive structure from the board level to operations level including job descriptions. While on strategy and structure, change was identified as something the board has to deal with. Different forms of change were discussed and the role of the board in change governance was highlighted and the McKinsey 7 S model was proposed as a tool the board could use in ensuring that organizational change remains consistent with desired outcomes. That the board is ultimately accountable for the success or failure of change was emphasized through coverage of risk management. The chapter concluded by discussing business continuity risk and the criticality of succession planning.

QUESTIONS AND EXERCISES

1. Discuss the relationship between leadership ethics and integrity and corporate governance.
2. Discuss the main corporate governance issues linked to business continuity and CEO succession.
3. SMEs do not need a board of directors but need corporate governance mechanisms that come with having an effective board. Discuss giving specific examples.
4. Organization design is the core of corporate governance for SMEs and or entrepreneurial firms. Discuss making reference to organizations you have worked with.

REFERENCES AND FURTHER READING

1. Adams, J., Bailey Jr, D. E., Anderson, R.A. & Galanos, A. N., (2013). Adaptive leadership: a novel approach for family decision-making. *Journal of palliative medicine*, *16*(3), 326–329.

2. Anderson, D. & Anderson, L. A., (2010). *Beyond change management: How to achieve breakthrough results through conscious change leadership*. John Wiley & Sons.

3. Appelbaum, S. H., Nadeau, D. & Cyr, M., (2008). Performance evaluation in a matrix organization: a case study (Part One). *Industrial and Commercial Training*, *40*(5), 236–241.

4. Appelbaum, S. H., Nadeau, D. and Cyr, M., 2008. Performance evaluation in a matrix organization: a case study (Part Two). *Industrial and Commercial Training*, *40*(6), 295–299.

5. Bamford, D. R., & Forrester, P. L., (2003). Managing planned and emergent change within an operations management environment. *International Journal of Operations and Production Management*, *23*(5), 546–564.

6. Banerji, P. & Krishnan, V. R., (2000). Ethical preferences of transformational leaders: An empirical investigation. *Leadership and Organization Development Journal, 21*(8), 405–413.

7. Banutu-Gomez, M.B. & Banutu-Gomez, S. M., (2016). Organizational Change and Development. *European Scientific Journal, 12*(22).

8. Benn, S., Dunphy, D. & Griffiths, A., (2014). *Organizational Change for Corporate Sustainability*. Routledge.

9. Bennington, G., (2000). Deconstruction and ethics. In *Deconstructions* (pp. 64–82). Palgrave, London.

10. Bills, K. L., Lisic, L.L. & Seidel, T. A., (2016). Do CEO Succession and Succession Planning Affect Stakeholders' Perceptions of Financial Reporting Risk? *Evidence from Audit Fees. The Accounting Review.*

11. Brightman, B. K. & Moran, J. W., (2001). Managing organizational priorities. *Career Development International*, *6*(5), 244–288.

12. Burke, W. W., (2013). *Organization Change: Theory and Practice*. Sage Publications.

13. Burnes, B., (2004). Kurt Lewin and the planned approach to change: a re-appraisal. *Journal of Management Studies*, *41*(6), 977–1002.

14. Burton, R. M., Obel, B. & Håkonsson, D. D., (2015). How to get the

Matrix Organization to Work. *Journal of Organization Design*, *4*(3), 37–45.

15. Clegg, S., Kornberger, M. & Rhodes, C., (2007). Business ethics as practice. *British Journal of Management, 18(2)*, 107–122.

16. Covin, J. G. & Slevin, D. P., (1988). The influence of organization structure on the utility of an entrepreneurial top management style. *Journal of management studies, 25*(3), 217–234.

17. Cummings, T. G. & Huse, E. F., (1989). Organizational Development and Change, West Publishers: St Paul.

18. De Jong, G., Tu, P. A. & van Ees, H., (2012). Which entrepreneurs bribe and what do they get from it? Exploratory evidence from Vietnam. *Entrepreneurship Theory and Practice, 36*(2), 323–345.

19. Deschamps, J. & Nelson, B., (2013). Governing Innovation in Practice– The Role of the Board of Directors. Innovation Management. se http://www.innovationmanagement. se/2013/05/21/governinginnovation-in-practice-the-role-of-the-board-of-directors.

20. Deschamps, J. P., (2013). What is innovation governance? – Definition and scope. www.InnovationManagement.se.

21. Deschamps, J. P., & Nelson, B., (2014). Innovation governance: how top management organizes and mobilizes for innovation. *Management, 42*, 3.

22. Dunphy, D. & Stace, D. A. (1993). The strategic management of corporate change. *Human Relations*, *46*(8), 905–920.

23. Eilat, Y. & Zinnes, C., (2002). The shadow economy in transition countries: Friend or foe? A policy perspective. *World Development, 30*(7), 1233–1254.

24. Fugate, M., (2012). The impact of leadership, management, and HRM on employee reactions to organizational change. *Research in Personnel and Human Resources Management, 31*(1), 177–208.

25. Gilding, M., Gregory, S. & Cosson, B., (2015). Motives and outcomes in family business succession planning. *Entrepreneurship Theory and Practice, 39*(2), 299–312.

26. Gnan, L., Montemerlo, D. & Huse, M., (2015). Governance systems in family SMEs: The substitution effects between family councils and corporate governance mechanisms. *Journal of Small Business Management, 53*(2), 355–381.

27. Gosling, J. & Mintzberg, H., (2003). The five minds of a manager. *Harvard Business Review, 81*(11), 54–63.

28. Handy, C., (1989). *The Age of Unreason.* Arrow Books: London.

29. Hawkins, J., (2016), August, 9. Making your business more successful with a leadership development program. http://www.forbes.com/sites/forbescoachescouncil/2016/08/09/making-your-business-more-successful-with-a-leadership-development-program/#686b4c911146.

30. Holder-Webb, L., Cohen, J. R., Nath, L., & Wood, D., (2009). The supply of corporate social responsibility disclosures among US firms. *Journal of Business Ethics, 84*(4), 497–527.

31. Jones, C., (2003). *As if Business Ethics were Possible, within Such Limits' Organization, 10*(2), 223–248.

32. Kaler, J., (2000). Reasons to be ethical: Self-interest and ethical business. In Business Challenging Business Ethics: New Instruments for Coping with Diversity in International Business (pp. 161–173). Springer Netherlands.

33. Kanter, R. M., Stein, B. A., & Jick, T. D., (1992). *The Challenge of Organizational Change.* New York: The Tree Press.

34. Kanter, R. M., (1984). *Change Masters.* Simon & Schuster.

35. Kanter, R. M., (2003). Challenge of organizational change: How companies experience it and leaders guide it. Simon & Schuster.

36. Kanter, R. M., (2012). Ten reasons people resist change. *Harvard Business Review Blog, 25.*

37. Kavanagh, M. H. & Ashkanasy, N. M., (2006). The impact of leadership and change management strategy on organizational culture and individual acceptance of change during a merger. *British Journal of Management, 17*(S1), pp. S81–S103.

38. Kessler, S. R., Nixon, A. E., & Nord, W. R. (2017). Examining Organic and Mechanistic Structures: Do We Know as Much as We Thought?. *International Journal of Management Reviews, 19*(4), 531-555.

39. Kotter, J. P., (1996). *Leading Change.* Harvard Business Press.

40. Kotter, J., (1999). Change leadership. *Executive Excellence, 16*(4), 16–17.

41. Kotterman, J., (2006). Leadership versus management: what's the difference?. *The Journal for Quality and Participation, 29*(2), 13.

42. Kraus, S., Harms, R. & Schwarz, E., (2008). Strategic business planning and success in small firms. *International Journal of Entrepreneurship and Innovation Management*, *8*(4), 381–396.

43. Larcker, D. F., & Tayan, B. (2016). CEO Succession Planning. *The Handbook of Board Governance: A Comprehensive Guide for Public, Private and Not for Profit Board Members*, 141-158.Lemke, D.K. & Schminke, M., (1991). Ethics in declining organizations. *Business Ethics Quarterly*, 235–248.

44. Luecke, R., (2003). *Managing Change and Transition* (Vol. 3). Harvard Business Press.

45. Marks, M. L. & Mirvis, P. H., (2011). A framework for the human resources role in managing culture in mergers and acquisitions. *Human Resource Management*, *50*(6), 859–877.

46. Mathis, K. & Shannon, D., (2009). Jeremy Bentham's Utilitarianism. *Efficiency Instead of Justice?*, 103–119.

47. Mintzberg, H., (1993). *Structure in fives: Designing Effective Organizations*. Prentice-Hall, Inc.

48. Mullins, W. & Schoar, A., (2016). How do CEOs see their roles? Management philosophies and styles in family and non-family firms. *Journal of Financial Economics*, *119*(1), 24–43.

49. Nica, E., (2013). Organizational culture in the public sector. *Economics, Management and Financial Markets*, *8*(2), 179.

50. O'Fallon, M. J. & Butterfield, K. D., (2005). A review of the empirical ethical decision-making literature: 1996–2003. *Journal of Business Ethics*, *59*(4), 375–413.

51. Osborn, R. N., Hunt, J.G. & Jauch, L. R., (2002). Toward a contextual theory of leadership. *The Leadership Quarterly*, *13*(6), 797–837.

52. Quinn, R. W. & Quinn, R. E. (2016). Change management and leadership development have to mesh. *Harvard Business Review,* 7 January. Retrieved from *https://hbr.org/2016/01/change-management-and-leadership-development-have-to-mesh*.Ready, D. A. (2016). 4 things successful change leaders do well. *Harvard Business Review,* 28 January. Retrieved from *https://hbr.org/2016/01/4-things-successful-change-leaders-do-well*.

53. Rutherford, M. W., Buller, P. F. & Stebbins, J. M., (2009). Ethical considerations of the legitimacy lie. *Entrepreneurship Theory and Practice*, *33*(4), 949–964.

54. Stanford, N., (2007). *Guide to Organization Design: Creating High-Performing and Adaptable Enterprises* (Vol. 10). John Wiley & Sons.

55. Todnem By, R., (2005). Organizational change management: A critical review. *Journal of Change Management, 5*(4), 369–380.

56. Vakola, M., Armenakis, A. & Oreg, S., (2013). Reactions to organizational change from an individual differences perspective: A review of empirical research. *The Psychology of Organizational Change: Viewing Change from the Employee's Perspective*, 95–122.

57. Van de Ven, A.H. & Poole, M. S., (1995). Explaining development and change in organizations. *Academy of Management Review, 20*(3), 510–540.

58. Van de Ven, A.H. & Poole, M. S., (2005). Alternative approaches for studying organizational change. *Organization Studies, 26*(9), 1377–1404.

59. Webb, J. W., Tihanyi, L., Ireland, R. D., & Sirmon, D. G., (2009). You say illegal, I say legitimate: Entrepreneurship in the informal economy. *Academy of Management Review, 34*(3), 492–510.

60. Wilden, R., Gudergan, S. P., Nielsen, B. B., & Lings, I., 2013. Dynamic capabilities and performance: strategy, structure and environment. *Long Range Planning, 46*(1), 72–96.

7
CHAPTER

FAIRNESS AND TRANSPARENCY

Chapter Aims and Objectives

By the end of this chapter, you would have learned about fairness and transparency as two of the five components of SME corporate governance. You would have covered the following:

Fairness in employee relations with;

- Executive compensation
- Discipline and grievance procedures
- Workplace democracy
- Fundamental elements of employee relations
- International context – the International Labor Organization (ILO)
- Industrial democracy
- Organizational justice – procedural, distributive and interactional justice

Transparency

- Recruitment and promotion
- Job evaluation and job analysis
- Grade based pay structure

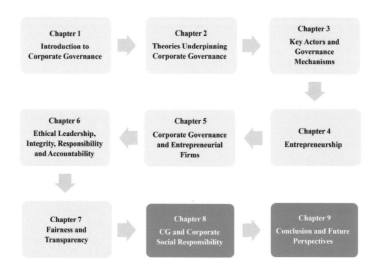

7.1. INTRODUCTION

Fairness and transparency speak to stakeholder relations and fostering trust. This starts with identification of the company's stakeholders. These include shareholders, investors, employees, creditors, debtors, investors, customers, the media and the community at large. Each one of the stakeholders has both legitimate and non-legitimate expectations, which an SME must always be aware of. Suitable policies and strategies must be developed to facilitate ongoing engagement in order to maintain positive relationships and to build trust and confidence with the critical stakeholders. The Board or its equivalent is responsible for balancing the varying interests ensuring that the interests of the company are safe guarded given that stakeholder perceptions can impact performance. As part of good practice the Board or its equivalent should ensure that management reports on environmental sustainability and social responsibility issues as part of their financial reporting.

Employees, communities in which businesses operate and environmentalists are among the key stakeholder groups affected by organizational fairness. This chapter focuses on employees. Fairness and transparency issues concerning the community will be handled in the next chapter. Employee fairness relates to compensation, workplace democracy, growth opportunities, work-life balance, and respect or protection of their rights.

7.2. COMPENSATION

Fairness and transparency in employees' compensation hinge on the organization's rewards philosophy which represents the fundamental beliefs and values that determine an organization's attitude towards the remuneration of its workers. It is the responsibility of the board or its equivalent to clearly articulate remuneration guidelines that management implement in a transparent manner. The rewards philosophy may cover topics such as given in the following subsections.

7.2.1. Organization's Pay Scale Position

What is critical in the organization's pay scale position is not so much what the organization pays but rather what the basis for the payment is. When compared to other similar organizations what is the organization's targeted pay scale position? Is it to be among the top quartile payers or among those in the median or among the lower quartile payers? In the example illustrated in Table 7.1 the 90th percentile indicates that only 10% of organizations pay at that level, 75th means 25% pay at that level or more while the rest pay less, 50th means 50% pay more than that level while 25th means 75% of organization pay more than that level or that 25% pay at that level. The Board provides guidance for the level to be adopted by a company based on its remuneration philosophy and ability to pay. Management has been known to want organizations to pay at the 75th percentile when organizational performance does not support such a move. Adopting a clear policy makes it less difficult for the organization to manage the expectations of employees as at any given time one is able to check on pay ranges in the market and determine whether or not they are being treated fairly. Where there is no clear policy on the organization's position dissatisfaction and unwarranted employee turnover may result.

Table 7.1: Pay Scales Comparisons

Position	90th	75th	50th	25th
CEO	25000–35000	20000–24999	15000–19999	10000–14999
COO	20000–24999	15000–19999	12000–14999	9000 – 14999
FD	20000–24999	18000–19999	15000–17999	9000 – 14999
HR	18000–19999	15000–17999	9000 – 14999	5000–8999
Marketing	18000–19999	15000–17999	9000 – 14999	7000–8999

7.2.2. Transparency of Rewards

Transparency of rewards means employees knowing how their salaries are determined and having comfort in knowing that there is equity in the payment of salaries. Transparency of rewards means that employees doing jobs in the same grade or level are paid within the same salary range or structure. Salary structures that are transparent are achieved through having jobs that are graded using an accepted method. Job evaluation is used to arrive at such structures.

Job evaluation is the process of determining the relative worth of jobs based on their descriptions. There are four broad types of job evaluation systems: decision bands, ranking, points based systems and factor comparison based systems. The process of job evaluation is covered in more detail later in this chapter, for the moment suffice to state that it involves three main steps which are:

- Collecting data on the job using. This is usually obtained from both the job incumbent and the supervisor;
- Analyzing the job in order to identify its main duties, the decisions it makes, its consequences of error and the basic qualifications and experience required to perform it at acceptable levels;
- Grading or classifying the job activities and requirements using pre-agreed standards resulting in the allocation of a grade.

Once all jobs have been allocated grades they are grouped according to grade and a salary structure is developed. The salary structure is a matrix that illustrates the levels of pay in an organization from the lowest paid position to the highest (Table 7.2). The structure is developed guided by the economic conditions both current and projected, the relative value of jobs as per the job evaluation and job grading, the results of an analysis of levels of salaries of similar jobs in the market, and the organization's reward philosophy. Through it, while an employee may not know another's actual salary they know the range within which it falls.

A pay structure provides clarity to the market and internal value of jobs making it possible to effectively communicate with employees and for them to know that they are paid equitably. Equitable in this case does not mean that employees receive similar amounts for the same job but rather that they all know the range within which their salaries fall regardless of differences they may have as a result of years in service and experience. For managers it improves the governance of employee remuneration because at any given time the highest possible salary bill can be worked out from the salary structure. Further, when recruiting a manager has guidance in terms of where to peg an employee's salary.

Table 7.2: Job Grading Based Salary Scale

Grade	Positions	Scale
1	Group CEO	35000–39999
2	Managing Directors COO Group Finance Director	25000–34999
3	Senior Managers HR Marketing Production Finance Manager	20000–24999
4	Middle level Management Specialists	15000–19999
5	Professionals/Officers	10000–14999

7.2.2.1. Equal Pay for Equal Effort

Where job evaluation ensures that there is an equal pay range for jobs graded as having the same worth, it does not account or reward different levels of performance. Where no governance mechanisms are in place to address differences in this area, an organizational slowly drops to posting mediocre performance. This aspect is addressed through performance management and performance-based pay resulting in variable pay within the same grade. This is an area where transparency and fairness are required as poor governance in the area can lead to workplace unrest.

Variable pay for effort is usually in the form of merit increases to the base salary, individual and group performance bonus; profit sharing; gain sharing and commission. The Board has to decide on the combination of payments that further the interests of the business without necessarily short changing the employees. Companies usually use a mixture of plans based on what they would be trying to achieve. The important thing therefore is knowing what the variable pay is intended to communicate and ensuring that it does not communicate the unintended. Variable pay structuring involves balancing focusing on the individual employee and on both the immediate team and the whole organization. That balancing act largely lies with the Board as management tends to be conflicted.

Equal pay for equal effort means employees performing at the same level and who are in the same grade must be paid the same amount. Payment for individual performance comes in the form of salary increase based on merit, performance-based bonus, contribution pay and skills based pay. Each one of these forms of pay has implications which the Board of business leader needs to be aware of in its compensation governance mechanisms.

Merit-based salary increase: Merit-based pay is linked to the performance appraisal process. It targets the individual employee and is usually paid in the form of a salary increase within an existing salary scale. The amount of the increase is varies to distinguish different levels of employee performance. The increases are usually implemented annually following a formal performance management process. Two governance issues arise from merit-based pay. Firstly is the need for a transparent process of translating performance ratings, points or grades into a salary figure. Table 7.3 illustrates a possible way of converting from a performance grade to a salary figure.

Table 7.3: Allocation of Performance-based Salary Increase

Position: Sales Executive Position Grade: 5 Salary Scale: $2500 – $3500 increasing in $125 notches				
NAME	Current Salary	Performance rating	Notches	New Salary
Tom	2500	A	3	2875
Alice	2500	B	2	2750
John	2500	C	1	2625
Sarah	2750	D	0	2750

Since merit pay is added to the base salary, in the long-term it can distinguish high performers from average and poor performers. Its being cumulative, however, presents the second governance challenge. Because the increase is cumulative the organization has to carry the same salary expense even during periods when an employee's performance drops to unacceptable levels. Managers have been known to abuse such a facility for their own advantage.

7.2.2.2. Performance-based Bonus

A performance bonus is a lump sum pre-agreed amount that is paid to an employee following the attainment of specific goals. A performance bonus can be either individual, immediate team or group based depending on the circumstances at hand and the message the organization seeks to communicate through the payment. The amount the bonus can vary depending on company guidelines. The bonus can be distributed equally among team members, distributed according to individual contribution or according to salary differences so that the bonus is paid as a proportion of one's actual salary. Governance issues on bonuses relate to ensuring that there is alignment between such payments and the overall strategic intentions of the business. Where there are inadequate governance mechanisms such bonuses have resulted in dysfunctional behavior. The Board has to ensure that bonus payments do not encourage high-levels of risk-taking.

7.2.2.3. Contribution Pay

These are instances when a company is not performing well financially yet there are employees who would have made significant contribution in terms of their contribution that would enhance future performance. The payment is once-off.

7.2.2.4. Skills Based Pay

Skill-based pay is based on the need to reward employees who would have acquired required skills that would improve their future performance. The payment is added to the employee's base pay either as a standalone allowance, for example critical skills allowance, or is added in the form of moving the employee several notches up the applicable pay scale.

7.2.2.5. Profit-Sharing

Profit sharing involves employees getting a share of the company's profits based on some pre-agreed formula. In listed companies profit sharing can also be in the form of employees being allocated shares in the company. It is one area that needs close governance as it has been found to lead to over focusing on short-term gains at the expense of solid long-term performance. A better approach more consistent with organizational objectives is gain-gain sharing. In the case of gain-sharing employees get additional payment based on gains that are made as a result of for example operational cost savings.

7.2.2.6. Total Rewards – Looking Beyond Basic Pay

When considering employee rewards the board has to look beyond basic pay. Guidance has to be given in terms of for example what percentage of the total pay are allowances or other benefits; what maximum profit sharing and or bonus is payable; and what happens during lean years where employees perform at acceptable levels but the business is still not generating sufficient profits.

An organization's rewards philosophy aims at enabling it to attract, motivate and retain the right skills to ensure successful implementation of its strategic objectives without inadvertently facilitating dysfunctional behavior (Table 7.4).

Table 7.4: Summary Aims of a Formal Rewards Philosophy

Aims of reward management
• Support the achievement of business goals by developing a performance culture and stimulating high performance;
• Clarify what is important in terms of behaviors and outcomes;
• Alignment with employee needs;
• Rewarding people according to their contribution value they create;
• Attracting and retaining high-quality people needed for strategy implementation
• Motivate employee to high performance
• Increase levels of employee engagement, commitment and loyalty
• Add value to employees through learning and growth opportunities
• Alignment with pay systems with types of people and their preferences

Through the strategic management of rewards employees are rewarded in a manner that enables them to focus on delivering organizational value that exceeds what they cost the organization.

The rewards philosophy of an organization is influenced by its Vision and Mission both of which are derived from the board. The rewards philosophy is a reflection of the vision, mission and the strategic objectives. The board has to ensure that the reward philosophy is aligned to the strategy being pursued during the life span of a specific plan. An organization that is on a growth trajectory will have a rewards philosophy different from one that is stagnating or retrenching. An organization's chosen basis for competing also affects the rewards philosophy. An organization that is set on using talent as its major source of competitive advantage will have a reward philosophy different from the one whose basis for competing is its non-human resources. A rewards philosophy that is not aligned to the vision, mission and strategic objectives results in a burdensome rewards budget that becomes a liability and may eventually lead to employees' retrenchment which in itself is indicative of a failure in governance. Figure 7.1 illustrates examples of rewards philosophies. Takeda Canada has a philosophy of recognizing and rewarding strong performance while Stanford has one of attracting, retaining and rewarding high performers at all levels.

Total Rewards Philosophy

Takeda Canada supports a Total Rewards philosophy that rewards and recognizes strong performance. Our highly successful model consists of a mix of performance : base pay, variable pay programs, a competitive benefits and perquisites program, work-life balance initiatives, rewards and recognition programs, and learning and development opportunities.

http://www.takedacanada.com/join-us/total-rewards-philosophy/

Our Compensation Philosophy

Stanford is committed to providing a fair and competitive staff compensation program that will attract, retain and reward high-performing employees at all levels. The university is also committed to providing a total staff compensation package tied to the attainment of individual and group results and the achievement of organizational goals.

Primary principles that guide our staff compensation program

- Pay what a job is worth.
- Recognize and reward individual and group performance.

https://cardinalatwork.stanford.edu/benefits-rewards/compensation/staff-compensation/our-compensation-philosophy

Figure 7.1: Rewards philosophy.

Beyond the vision mission and strategic objectives, the core business of an organization, its culture, structure and ability to pay also influences the rewards philosophy, with technical and scientific organizations being more likely to pay for skills held than for actual work performed. The prevailing culture in the organization both influences and is influenced by the rewards philosophy. There is a two way relationship between culture and rewards philosophy. For example, a desire to have a high performance culture will be reflected in the rewards philosophy. An organization with a tall structure may have a philosophy of paying for years in service yet one with flat structure is more likely to have a philosophy of for example paying for performance.

Finally ability to pay in the long-term can influence an organization's pay philosophy as it has to pay in line with what it can afford in a sustainable manner.

Where a board fails to appreciate these various influences, key skills could be lost exposing the organization to the risk of failing to execute its chosen strategy. Rewards philosophy is a critical company governance issue. In the interest of fairness and transparency the board has to address the questions:

- What type of human capital resources will we need to execute our plans at a level that will guarantee us the desired results?
- How much should the resources cost us?
- How should we structure the cost so that it is aligned to our achieving the objectives?

Responses to these high-level questions inform the main components of the reward system which are:

- Determination of the base salary: a process which will be illustrated in subsequent sections.
- Determination of the magnitude of contingent pay if applicable – how much or what percentage of the salary will be open to risk?
- Determination of non-salary benefits both financial and non-financial.
- Determination of performance management based component.
- Total cost of employment or total rewards.

A depiction of the system is given in Figure 7.2.

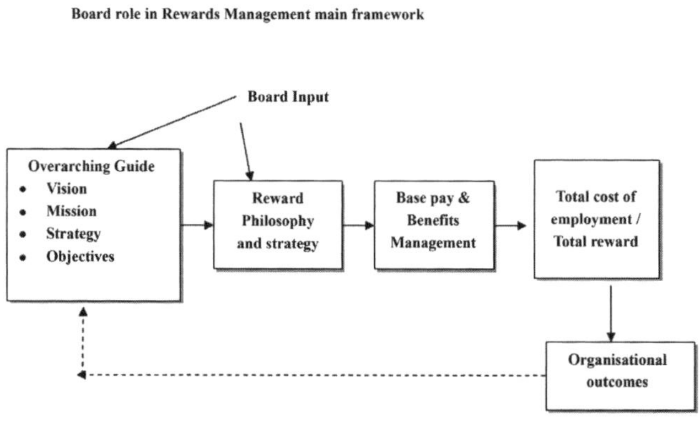

Board role in Rewards Management main framework

Figure 7.2: Reward management system.

7.3. EXECUTIVE COMPENSATION

While the board provides the broad framework for rewards management in an organization, it is responsible for the detailed structuring of the remuneration of the CEO and executive management's compensation. The management of the rewards of the rest of the employees in an organization gets its direction from that of the CEO and executives. Aligning executive compensation to the business strategic deliverables is a critical component of executive attraction and retention and is at the same time at the core of corporate governance.

7.3.1. Agency Theory and Executive Pay

Executive compensation is grounded in Agency theory as it explains the relationship between shareholders and executives and addresses the inherent conflict in the relationship between the two. The shareholder expects the executives to maximize the value of their investment and in return be compensated in line with achievement of goals. In practice executives are risk averse and focus only engage in activities that are not likely to expose them to failure without necessarily maximizing shareholder value.

Agency theory explains the contractual relationship between the business owner (principal, and the executive (agent). The principal has the capital but not the skills and therefore hires an agent who has the skills but not the capital. The principal is assumed to be risk neutral and is only interested in getting maximum return on the investment. The agent, on the other hand, is assumed to be self-serving only interested in those activities that do not expose him/her to unnecessary risk. Based on these assumptions it becomes obvious that, the agent wants to put in minimum possible effort while being paid the maximum possible while the principal wants the agent to give more for less pay. Agency theory addresses this inherent conflict in the relationship (Harris and Bromiley, 2007; Dalton et al., 2007). This conflict of interest is what is referred to as the agency problem and is at the root of the executive motivation problem faced by business owners. Overall agency theory as espoused by both Ross (1973), focusing on incentives, and Mitnick (2013), focusing on institutional structures, seeks to resolve problems that potentially arise when the wishes of the principal and those of the agent conflict and it is either impossible or not cost-effective for the principal to check on the work of the agent to ensure that it is in line with what was agreed. It also seeks to address problems of risk sharing that arise when the two contracting parties have differences in risk appetites which could result in the parties preferring different courses of action (Eisenhardt, 1989).

Agency loss, which is the difference between the ideal outcome for the principal and the results of the actions of the agent, has been found to be reduced in situations where the principal and the agent pursue common outcomes; the principal has full knowledge of the outcomes expected from the agent; and pay is in line with the agent's effort exertion based on freely available measures (Roberts, 2004).

A typical executive package includes base pay, annual incentives, bonuses, stock grants, stock options, other forms of compensation and benefits. The intention is for the executive, as the agent, to get adequate compensation to encourage them to adequately represent the interests of shareholders (Bebchuk and Fried, 2003). Base Pay is the guaranteed financial reward received by an executive. The quantum of the base pay is usually determined by the Board through benchmarking using industry salary surveys or executive pay consultants. Incentives that are paid annually are usually in the form of performance linked annual bonus plans which are paid in cash or shares or both. The performance that guides this award is as reflected in the business' financial reports. Components of executive pay and their rationale are discussed in turn below.

7.3.1.1. Basic Pay

Basic Pay is the guaranteed pay given to an executive for work done. It excludes any other benefits. The base salary of an executive is usually determined by the Board through benchmarking based on industry salary surveys. This is not without problems and these will be discussed in the next section.

7.3.1.2. Annual Incentives

Annual incentives are usually in the form of performance linked annual Bonus Plans paid in cash or shares or both. The performance referred to is as reflected in the firm's accounting reports.

7.3.1.3. Executive Share Option Scheme (ESOS)

Executives usually also participate in Executive Share Option Schemes (ESOS) which is an arrangement where executives are given the option to buy the firm's shares at a fixed price at a future date. The intention of ESOS is to align the medium to long-term interests of the executives with those of shareholders in order to prevent them from activities that may bring short-term positive results while eroding long-term value. In some instances these may account for as much as 60% to 70% of an executive's compensation (Ebert, Torres and Papadakis, 2008). ESOS are not without problems as they have been associated with executives taking excessive risks, focusing on short-term benefits, postponing of dividend payment, manipulating financial reporting, and costing the firm more than the value attached to them (Bognanno, 2010; Dong, Wang, and Xie, 2010). Increases in financial reporting irregularities have also been associated with the introduction of ESOS (Efendi, Srivastava and Swanson, 2007).

7.3.1.4. Long-Term Incentives

Long-term incentives are based on the long-term performance of a business and include schemes such as restricted shares tied to the executive's tenure; vested and restricted stock bonuses tied to achievement of specified targets or attainment of specific milestones and the already discussed ESOS. The long-term incentives are meant to prevent executives from engaging in behavior detrimental to long-term shareholder interests (Chen, Pelger, and Sandmann, 2013).

7.3.1.5. Lump Sum Payments

Executive pay also has lump sum payments meant to cover various eventualities all in the interest of addressing the agency problem, for example, golden parachutes. Originating in the 1980s at the height of mergers and acquisitions, this is a lump sum payment made to an executive following termination of an employment contract as a result of a firm takeover or a merger. While some view it as critical in enabling a business to attract and retain talented executives others view it as guaranteeing executives pay for failure (Fich, Tran, and Walkling, 2013).

7.3.2. Critical Issues in Executive Pay

Academic explanations of trends in executive pay have followed two paths: the efficient contracting group and the managerial power group. The efficient contracting group is of the view that the levels and composition of executive pay are a reflection of competitive equilibrium in the market for executive talent and are structured to provide maximum value to the business by addressing agency problems. The managerial power group view pay levels and composition as a reflection of board members who have fallen victim to the whims of powerful CEOs (Bebchuk and Fried, 2003) and therefore as indicative of agency problems between the board and the shareholders. Frydman and Jenter (2010) found both managerial power and competitive market forces to be important determinants of executive pay but with none of them being individually supported by existing evidence.

The underpinning of executive compensation in agency theory has presented challenges in the need to attract and retain motivated executives while paying attention to critical issues that include balancing attracting and retaining motivated executives and linking pay with performance; determination of the ideal pay level; magnitude of difference between executive pay and the next level; addressing inherent constraints that characterize executive contracts; going beyond executive market fallacies; interpretation and appropriate contextualization of benchmarking data; dealing with distributive justice issues emanating from pay dispersion and handling socio-political implications of the perceived inequity of executive pay.

The grounding of executive remuneration in agency theory has presented challenges such as:

- Balancing attracting and retaining motivated executives and the need to link pay to performance;
- Determination of the ideal pay level inherent constraints that characterize executive contracts;
- Magnitude of difference between executive pay and the next level and related distributive justice issues;
- Overcoming executive market fallacies;
- Interpretation and appropriate use of benchmarking data;
- Dealing with socio-political implications of the perceived inequity of executive pay.

7.3.2.1. Balancing Attracting, Retaining With Pay to Performance

Balancing the focus on attracting and retaining motivated executives with the need to link their pay to performance remains a challenge. Although over the years there phenomenal increases in executive pay have been attributed to the onset of performance related incentives there is lack of empirical evidence of a direct link between executive performance-based pay and business performance as executives have limited control over the results for which they are rewarded (Lorsch and Khurana, 2010). Performance Pay programs seek to remunerate executives based on performance which is ordinarily gauged using financial measures such as earnings per share. The outcome-based measures of performance seek to transfer the risk from the shareholder to the executive and the higher the transferred perceived or real risk, the higher the executive compensation (Eisenhardt, 1989). Several studies have highlighted the ineffectiveness of rewards that are focused on external factors (Pfeffer, 1998).

Pay for performance is based on motivation models driven by an assumption that the effectiveness of executives is directly related to the monetary rewards they get for their contribution. In reality executives have been found to have limited control over the results for which they are rewarded with organizational performance reflecting the performance of more people than just the executive (Lorsch and Khurana, 2010). Lack of clear evidence of a link between pay and performance continues to lead to questions on the justification for the high-levels of executive pay. The assumption that people are self serving and can be bribed into desired action has not been matched by empirical data, instead pay for performance programs have been found to influence executive decision-making in areas such as diversification; spend on research and development, strategic choices and investment decisions (Reynes and Gerhart, 2000); and dysfunctional behavior, as some executives end up focusing on working the system as was in the case of Enron (Welbourne, 2004).

7.3.2.2. Determination of the Ideal Pay Level

Determination of the ideal level of an executive's compensation package is problematic. This is usually based on an assumed existence of a market for executives where hiring organizations have to undertake competitive benchmarking in order to attract the right caliber of executive. This view is refuted by Lorsch and Khurana (2010) who argue that the level of the package is a product of the executive's ability to bargain. At the inception of an executive contract the parties have different views on cognitive, social-psychological, informational, and incentive issues resulting in incomplete contracts and the efficiency of the executive pay being left dependent on ex-post bargaining conditions of the parties which tend to work in favor of the executive (Ferri and Maber, 2013) especially in the absence of a strong board.

7.3.2.3. Magnitude of Difference Between Executive Pay and the Next Level

The magnitude of the difference between executive pay and the next level in an organization is another challenge in executive reward management. Since the turn of the century there has been astronomical widening of the gap between executive pay and that of non-executive employees. In a study focusing on a ten year period covering six developed countries, Ebert, Torres and Papadakis (2008) found that over the period executive pay had moved times 71 times the wage of the average worker to 183 times the wage of the average worker without factoring in other executive long-term benefits such as shares. Including these moved the figures from 103 times to 521 times over the same ten year period. While pay systems such as total reward as illustrated above could promote employee engagement and motivation, the levels of executive pay in an organization affect perceptions of equity of other managers and employees.

Within an individual firm, executive pay affects how other managers and employees feel and perform so that when lower level managers perceive themselves as underpaid relative to the CEO it results in increased intention to leave the organization (Wade, O'Reilly, and Pollock, 2006). Such intentions work against the interests of the shareholder. External to the organization large pay differences attract the concerns of other stakeholders over issues of distributive justice and fairness of the magnitude of executive pay regardless of levels of performance (Walsh, 2008; Harris, 2009).

7.3.2.4. MARKET Fallacy and use of Competitive Benchmarking

The basis used for determining pay level is another critical issue in executive pay. This is driven by an assumption that there is a market out there for executives and an organization has to engage in competitive benchmarking to enable it to attract and retain the right caliber of executive (Bizjak, 2008). Because Boards get their guidance from the competitive benchmarking that is determined by consultants who are conflicted because of the client relationship with the executives, there is continuous increase of executive pay that is not backed by performance but only illustrates the power of executives in controlling decisions on their own pay (Bognanno, 2010).

7.3.2.5. Socio-Political Considerations

There has been increased public outcry over the high-levels of executive pay regardless of whether or not such pay was linked to any positive developments within the firm (Rost and Weibel, 2013). This has been compounded by the bailing out of businesses where executives were perceived to be over paid in spite of poor business performance which has been viewed as paying for failure (see Figure 7.3).

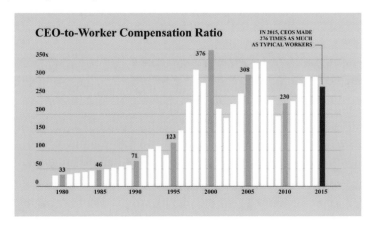

Figure 7.3: CEO – Workers compensation comparisons, Source: Lowenstein, R., 2017. CEO pay is out of control: Here's how to rein it in. http://fortune.com/2017/04/19/executive-compensation-ceo-pay/.

7.3.2.6. Corporate Governance and Executive Pay

Strengthening corporate governance structures helps address problems relating to executive pay and protecting the interests of the shareholders and of other stakeholders. This has been in the form of increasing the ratio of independent directors on boards and strengthening remuneration committees responsible for handling executive pay. Empirical evidence, however, does not point to any major improvements that can be attributed to these measures in both large organizations and SMEs.

A number of factors explain this situation.

First, independent directors are in fact not independent because in reality board members tend to be acquaintances of the CEO, who in fact has some influence on their appointment (Murphy, 2012). Second, there is information asymmetry with the remuneration committees usually not having adequate information to enable them to make more informed decisions on executive pay. To bridge the gap they rely on conflicted consultants. Out of a desire to look good the remuneration committees tend to accept the recommendations of consultants without much questioning.

Third, directors whether independent or not do not necessarily represent the interests of the shareholder. Directors are themselves another yet another agency problem as some board members more inclined to serve the personal interests of its members to the exclusion of those of the shareholders. This aspect is one of the factors that discourage SMEs from having "independent" directors who can potentially destroy their businesses.

7.3.2.7. Evaluation of Reward Systems

Another remuneration related corporate governance issue is the evaluation of pay systems as a way of ensuring that at any given time the system is aligned with the organization's strategy and is facilitating the attainment of the stated objectives. Brown and Reilly (2009) identified what they considered as the most important criteria for evaluating the effectiveness of a rewards strategy, these are:

- Convergence with the business strategy, required values, skill and behaviors;
- Paying for both contribution and performance;
- Extent of customization to suit the needs of different employees;
- Motivating employee and making them more committed;
- Sufficiently communicated, understood and valued by employees;
- Cost-effectiveness and affordability;
- Flexible enough to Change in response to changing needs;
- Ease with which it can be efficiently managed and administered;
- Compliance with the legal framework, internally equitable, and fair; and
- Externally competitive enough to facilitate recruitment and retention.

Despite the apparent criticality of evaluating an organization's pay system organizations, especially SMEs generally neglect this. According to Tropman (2002) an organization's pay system is the "elephant in the living room" and tends to remain unaddressed. In addressing why organizations do not evaluate their pay systems Armstrong, Brown and Reilly (2011) identified five popular reasons given in their order of popularity: lack of resources or time; lack of information or data; senior management indifference; organization changes; and lack of analytical skills. Management reluctance in cases is a result of their being conflicted and hence the need for the board to play a leading role as part of its governance responsibilities.

The board needs to regularly measure the effectiveness of a company pay system by setting the strategic reward objectives and success criteria, developing, implementing, reviewing, measuring and evaluating. Setting pay system objectives and success criteria incorporates setting the objectives of the pay management system and providing the basis of measuring achievement. The developing part focuses on coming up with pay structures and developing pay policies to guide the administration of the pay system. Implementation is the process of administering pay in line with the developed pay structures and salary scales. Reviewing involves making a comparison between practice and what was intended, and collecting data both internally and externally in order to conduct comparisons and to establish prevailing trends. Measurement involves collecting quantitative data relating to rewards while evaluation checks the impact of the system on other organizational processes.

7.4. FAIRNESS AND TRANSPARENCY IN EM-PLOYEE RELATIONS

Employee relations refer to relations between management as representatives of owners of a business and the employees. It incorporates the rules, regulations and agreements that are used in the management of employees both as individuals and as a collective. Employee relations cover all aspects of the relationship between the employer and employee and among employees including relations with collective bodies representing employees such as trade unions and workplace worker representatives. It therefore covers both collective and individual matters such as contracts of employment, workers as a collective, communication between the parties, handling of disagreements, grievances and disciplinary issues, employee perceptions of leadership style of the management team, employee engagement and diversity management.

The nature of employee relations impacts on organizational productivity with poor relations resulting in poor performance as a result of loss of focus, lack of teamwork, increase in dysfunctional behavior and time spent managing relational problems ranging from simple disagreement to collective action. The board has to ensure that management has put in place mechanisms that build employee commitment and engagement and reduce undesired turnover which could expose the organization to different risks.

Although many factors determine the nature of employee relations in an organization issues internal to the organization that are within the purview of the board and management are most relevant. Internal factors include: ownership structure and leadership and management style.

7.4.1. Fundamental Elements of Employee Relations

Internal fundamental elements of employee relations are: social justice, industrial democracy, and rights and responsibilities.

7.4.1.1. Social Justice

Social justice involves ensuring that employee fundamental rights are protected. These rights include:

- freedom of association;
- collective bargaining;
- right to join a trade union of own choice;
- right to participate or join a workers committee without fear of reprisal;
- barring any form of forced labor;
- prohibition of child labor;
- protection against any form of discrimination in the workplace;
- right to fair labor standards and a safe working environment and
- a democratic work environment.

7.4.1.2. Industrial Democracy

Industrial democracy is about workers participating in decision-making on matters that affect their work and the security of their jobs. This includes employee representation through trade unions, engaging in collective bargaining, having access to a grievance handling process, being consulted where necessary and other forms of participation.

7.4.1.3. Rights and Responsibilities

Both parties have rights and responsibilities. The employees have a right to a safe working environment, fair pay and working hours, fair share of profits, and participation in collective action. On the other hand they have the responsibility to produce at required levels while adhering to laid down regulations. Management has the right to hire, transfer, promote, discipline and fire, put in place rules and regulations and to conduct business in an enabling organizational atmosphere. Management has the responsibility to ensure that the business is operated profitably and to safeguard jobs.

7.5. INTERNATIONAL CONTEXT

In dealing with employee relations compliance issues the board needs to be mindful that employee relations are also enacted in the context of the rest of the world, specifically the International Labor Organization (ILO). The ILO is a tripartite U.N. agency that works with employers, worker representatives and governments towards setting labor standards, developing policies and devising programmes that promote decent work for all. The organization was established following the end of the First World War, premised on the belief that universal, lasting peace depends on its being based on social justice.

Since its inception the ILO has developed and continues to maintain a system of international labor standards the main of which include: removal of child and forced labor, barring discrimination in employment, ensuring freedom of association and collective bargaining and advancing opportunities for people to be engaged in decent and productive work where there is freedom, equity, security and dignity (http://www.ilo.org). The ILO standards provide a basic framework for minimum labor standards that ensure that everyone benefits from the global economy. The ILO does not have any powers to enforce the standards and relies on use of persuasion to get member states to comply. That notwithstanding, it is in the interest of the company that the board ensures compliance with the standards.

List of instruments by subject and status

Note : Withdrawn Conventions are closed for ratification.

1. Freedom of association, collective bargaining, and industrial relations

1.1. Fundamental Conventions on Freedom of association and collective bargaining

1.2. Freedom of association (agriculture, non-metropolitan territories)

1.3. Industrial relations

2. Forced labour

2.1. Fundamental Conventions on forced labour (and related Recommendations)

2.2. Other instruments on forced labour

3. Elimination of child labour and protection of children and young persons

3.1. Fundamental Conventions on child labour (and related Recommendations)

3.2. Protection of children and young persons

4. Equality of opportunity and treatment

4.1. Fundamental Conventions on equality of opportunity and treatment (and related Recommendations)

4.2. Workers with family responsibilities

5. Tripartite consultation

5.1. Governance Convention on tripartite consultation (and related Recommendation)

6. Labour administration and inspection

6.1. Governance Conventions on labour inspection (and related instruments)

P081 - Protocol of 1995 to the Labour Inspection Convention, 1947

R081 - Labour Inspection Recommendation, 1947 (No. 81)

R082 - Labour Inspection (Mining and Transport) Recommendation, 1947 (No. 82)

C129 - Labour Inspection (Agriculture) Convention, 1969 (No. 129)

R133 - Labour Inspection (Agriculture) Recommendation, 1969 (No. 133)

6.2. Other instruments on labour inspection

6.3. Labour administration

7. Employment policy and promotion

7.1. Governance Convention on employment policy (and related Recommendations)

7.2. Other instruments on employment policy and promotion

Figure 7.4: ILO Guidelines, *Source*: http://www.ilo.org/dyn/normlex/en/f?p=NORMLEXPUB:12030:0::NO.

The board and executive management set the tone of employee relations in an organization. Management can be divided into three broad categories: executive management and senior management and middle management. Each one of these play different roles although in all cases subject to the guidelines provided by the board and by regulatory authorities. Employee relations center on the use of power by its various holders. According to Sisson (2008) use of power in workplace relations is in two forms: power 'over' and power 'to'. The first form of power is something one party possesses over others, the board over the CEO and executive management, executive management over lower level management and the later over the generality of employees. The employment relationship is asymmetrical in that the employer and employee come to the table with one having more power over the other. The employer or the representative is in a more powerful position than the worker. "Power to" is the power one can to make specific decisions, set the agenda and to shape people's expectations (Lukes, 2005). All these forms of power impinge on employee relations and wrongly used lead to dysfunctional workplace relations.

In the exercise of "power over" and "power to" employee relations are affected by the need for democracy in the workplace. Part of fairness is observing the democratic rights of employees. Employee democracy is about the participation of employees in making decisions in the workplace. Other reasons for having employee democracy in the workplace are correcting power imbalances between employers and employees; extending democratic principles to workplaces; developing organizations that are responsive to community interests; fostering economic efficiency and co-operative work relationships (Gollan and Patmore, 2002).

Elements of workplace democracy include:

- Information sharing;
- Consultation;
- Codetermination
- Shared employer-employee commitment to achieving organizational success;
- Building trust through the recognition of every party's legitimate roles and interests;
- Attending to issues of quality of working life of the employees;
- Practice of granting equal opportunities and fair treatment of all employees;
- Addressing employment security in exchange for flexibility;
- Instituting quality improvement training interventions;
- Collaboration between employees and managers in solving workplace problems (Gollan and Patmore, 2002).

7.5.1. Information Sharing and Consultation

One of management's roles is to ensure that there is information sharing and consultation on issues. Employee relations in an organization are nurtured through ongoing communication through sharing relevant information and consultation on pertinent issues. Industrial disputes tend to emerge from information asymmetry and inadequate consultation.

Consultation is the process by which management and workers or representatives of both discuss issues of mutual interest which arise in the workplace. Management though still retains the prerogative to make the final decision having considered the contribution made by employees. Consultation should not be confused with collective bargaining as they are different. Collective bargaining is not a consultation process but rather a negotiation process where employers meet recognized employee representatives such as a trade union to negotiate pay and other terms of employment.

Communication and consultation are part of workplace democracy. Both processes are critical for good working relations especially when an organization is going through changes that impact on work processes and people's jobs. Managers are responsible for ensuring that there is continuous communication and consultation. Where management involves employees when making changes that affect their work, employees tend to accept the changes even when there could be some negative effect on them. Where management frequently excludes employees from such discussions, change tends to be resisted.

Communication and consultation have been associated with positive organizational developments such as improved decision-making, commitment, trust, job satisfaction, employee engagement, flexible working and work life balance, and improved performance. All levels of management are responsible for driving the communication and consultation processes in an organization. To be effective the processes need to be systematic spelling out areas of responsibility for communicating at different level of management in order to avoid confusion. It must be clear which level of management communicates or engages in consultation on which issues. Further, Trade Union leaders are also responsible for communicating specific information to their membership. Table 7.2 illustrates a summary of possible levels of communication in an organization.

Table 7.5: Levels of Responsibility for Communication

Management Level	Communication Responsibility
• Board	• Policy; vision, mission, overarching objectives

• Executive Management	• Policy – direction, vision, mission, strategic objectives
• Middle management and line management	• Cascading issues to staff and escalating issues to executive management
• Trade Union or Workers Committees as applicable	• Ensure member views are communicated to management

7.5.2. Specific Areas where There Must be Consultation

Areas that are subject to consultation will vary across organizations based on an organization's size, ownership, structure, extent of its centralization or decentralization, current and past employee relations climate, leadership and management style, what is to be discussed and the extent of involvement of trade unions. A communication and consultation policy gives guidance that assists in the maintenance of positive workplace relations. Such a policy needs to be monitored on a regular basis through for example: using external consultants to conduct an assessment of existing communication and consultation provisions; identify and discuss any additional organizational needs and institute improvement measures.

7.5.3. Co-Determination

Codetermination refers to the practice of workers having the right to vote for their own representatives to sit on the board of directors of the company they work for. The practice is common in Germany from where it originates. According to McGaughey (2014), in its most inclusive state:

"codetermination means not simply a right to vote for representatives on a board, but to have binding rights to vote on specific workplace issues, such as dismissals, work shift patterns, or social facilities, especially through a work council" (p.2).

Codetermination is practiced in various forms in different countries. In the UK it is practiced in the form of worker representatives' codetermination for pension plan trustees. In Sweden the Co-determination Act of 1977 covers a large number of rules including the right of association, the extended right of negotiation, the extended right to information, position of trade union representatives in the workplace, and private sector employees board representation (http://www.ikem.se/in_english/co-determination_at_the_workplace).

7.5.4. Trade Unions

Part of workplace democracy is employee right to associate through for example a Trade union. Trade Unions are organizations whose members are workers who have come together in order to represent their common interest with the principal purpose being that of negotiating for better wages and working conditions.

Employees join trade unions for a number of reasons but largely to use them as a way of negotiating for higher wages, better working conditions, protection from unfair dismissal or treatment, job security, social – relational needs, upgrading skills pressure from peers and self fulfillment that comes from participating in leadership positions within the trade union. The generic reason for joining trade unions is that collective action is more effective in advancing the common interests of employees than when dealt with at an individual level (Bennett and Kaufman, 2002).

7.5.6. Contracts of Employment

From a legal perspective, the employer–employee relationship is a contractual one. Theoretically the law assumes that in forming an agreement to be recognized at law (a contractual agreement) the employer and the employee have equal bargaining power; there is a promise to provide work in exchange for remuneration and the parties have their respective rights. In reality, however, employees approach the table with significantly less negotiating power than employers and employment contracts, being drafted by employers, do more to highlight the obligations of the employee and the rights of the employer. State involvement in the employer-employee relationship becomes important in this regard as it is the state which steps in to provide adequate protections to employees through various laws and regulations, even and especially where employees are not aware of their rights and employer obligations. Whilst it is not obligatory for a contract to be in writing there is a statutory minimum requirement that employers provide employees with written particulars of the main terms and conditions of employment. It is therefore good corporate governance to ensure that employees have written contracts. While in large organizations this may be a given, in SMEs the board has to ensure that employees, especially executives have written signed contracts. The contract adds transparency to the employer–employee relationship as it covers:

- Date of commencement of employment, and whether any previous service with the employer counts as continuous.

- Date of expiry of fixed contracts
- Holidays
- Job title and abridged description as well as location.
- Notice of termination
- Pension rights.
- Provision for sickness or injury
- Remuneration, rate and interval
- Terms of collective agreements affecting work conditions
- The names of the employer and employee.
- Working hours of work and normal working hours.

7.5.7. Grievances and Discipline

Other areas in employee relations that call for fairness and transparency are grievances and discipline.

A grievance arises when an employee perceives themselves as not having been treated fairly or justly by the employer. This could be a result of the employer violating the terms and conditions of an employment contract, being discriminatory in the treatment of employees or denying an employee a right they believe they deserve for example a promotion of salary increase. Like in the case of a disciplinary issue, in the first instance an attempt is made to solve a grievance informally, when this fails the formal grievance procedure route is taken. The process is summarized in Figure 7.5.

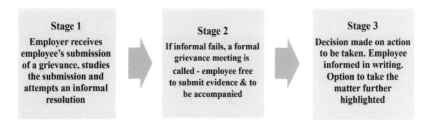

Figure 7.5: Grievance Procedure.

Corporate governance requires that employee discipline is guided by the laid down rules and standard operating procedures in the workplace usually documented in an organization's code of conduct. A typical code of conduct spells out the acts of misconduct and the penalties for any violations. The acts of misconduct are usually grouped according to their seriousness and the penalty they attract for example: into minor misconduct that results in a verbal warning, serious misconduct that may result in a written warning and gross misconduct that may result in instant dismissal or suspension. The main elements of an organization's disciplinary procedure are the existence of a code of conduct which every employee acknowledges being aware of by signing for it and having that proof stored in the employee's file; and a guide of the steps to be followed when the code is violated, the disciplinary procedures. The code of conduct is developed with the participation of employee mandated representatives and therefore is part of the terms of an employee's contract of employment. A code of conduct cannot contain any rules that amount to violating any parts of applicable labor legislation.

Typical rules found in a code of conduct relate to:
- Fulfillment of terms and conditions of the contract of employment;
- Conduct that is inconsistent with terms of the employment contract;
- Following set out work procedures;
- Time keeping;
- Adherence to health and safety measures;
- Abuse of organizational property;
- Substance abuse while in the workplace;
- Discriminatory tendencies;
- Bullying and sexual harassment;
- Theft and fraud.

Disciplinary procedures are used to enforce an organization's rules as reflected in the Code of Conduct. Although disciplinary procedures may differ from organization to organization they all have core elements which are:
- The procedure is stated in writing;
- The intention is to correct the undesired commission or omission with minimum disruption to work performance;
- The minimum possible corrective measure that can correct the situation is adopted;
- The focus is on the employee deriving lessons from the situation and improving going forward;
- Transparency, fairness, and consistency in application of the rules;

- Observation of confidentiality;
- Conducted with mutual respect and dignity;
- Employee has a right to be heard and to defend themselves;
- Employee has a right to appeal against a disciplinary decision;
- The appeal procedures are clearly stated.

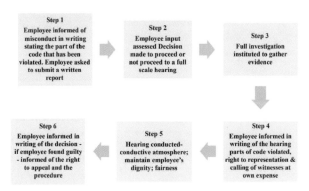

Figure 7.6: Disciplinary Process.

7.6. FRAMEWORK OF ORGANIZATIONAL JUSTICE

Organizational justice is about employees' perceptions of fairness in the workplace. Most grievances in the workplace stem from an employee feeling that there is lack of justice in the manner in which managers handle issues. This could lead into conflict, compromise performance and if left unattended precipitate different forms of dysfunctional behavior. Examples of injustice are:

- Being discriminated against in terms of pay level, benefits and access to training opportunities;
- Being denied privileges advanced to other employees in the same grade;
- Having a worse performer promoted ahead of a better performer;
- Inconsistencies in administering corrective action;
- Dismissal without justification.

There are three distinct forms of organizational justice that need to be addressed by governance structures: procedural, distributive and interactional.

7.6.1. Procedural Justice

Procedural justice is about the fairness of a decision-making process that leads to a specific outcome. For example, if an employee is to be dismissed, procedural justice is about whether the dismissal was handled in a manner consistent with the laid down procedures and the parts of the Code of Conduct being used to effect the dismissal. If it is a retrenchment exercise procedural justice is whether all the necessary steps were taken to get to identifying specific employee(s) to be the ones to lose their jobs. It is therefore not so much about the decision itself but rather about the process followed to get to the decision.

Factors that determine or contribute to organizational procedural justice are giving employees voice; morality and ethicality; recourse; accuracy of assumptions; and consistency.

7.6.1.1. Voice

Giving employees a chance to be heard so that they feel they participated in reaching the decision. Linked to this is the element of representativeness so that all those likely to be affected by a decision feel that they were consulted.

7.6.1.2. Morality and Ethicality

An assurance that the decisions taken had nothing to do with an employee's specific characteristics that had nothing to do with the job, for example, race, gender, age, nationality etc.

7.6.1.3. Recourse

This involves having the assurance that there are procedures for an employee to challenge a decision they dispute without fear of being victimized.

7.6.1.4. Accuracy of Assumptions

The assumptions and or information used to arrive at a decision must be seen to have been accurate at the time of making the decision. The decision must be seen to have been made solely on the basis of those accurate facts and not on other factors from the past with no direct bearing on the case in point.

7.6.1.5. Consistency

Similar situations and circumstances must always result in similar decisions without any exception.

7.6.2. Distributive Justice

Distributive justice addresses issues of equity. Through it, employees are able to feel that the organization is giving them a fair return for their contribution. Strike action and other forms of work stoppage and pilferage can be traced back to employee perception of distributive justice. What is critical in distributive justice is not the quantum of the rewards that is important but rather whether they are being distributed in an equitable manner. For example, there could be concerns on whether the performance management system is working well enough to enable the organization to distribute performance bonuses in a manner that distinguishes high performers from poor performers. Further, a concern could relate to other benefits are distributed in a manner that is consistent with whatever measure is in place for differentiating among employees in the same grade.

7.6.3. Interactional Justice

Interactional justice is about the manner in which management interacts with employees in terms of the extent to which there is: truthfulness, appropriateness, respect and dignity.

One of the commonest organizational justice issues relates to unfair dismissal and or constructive dismissal. The dismissal of an employee is considered unfair if it has any of the following characteristics:

- Implemented without following proper procedures as laid down in applicable guidelines. This is the most common form of unfair dismissal;
- As punishment for participating in trade union activities;
- As punishment for seeking redress against an employer's failure to implement employment rights;
- A female employee who is expecting a baby;
- dismissal for any reason excluded by anti-discrimination legislation;
- dismissal for taking part dismissal on grounds of pregnancy;
- For refusal to do shop or betting work on a Sunday;

- •   Refusing to be a member of a trade union;
- •   Refusing to follow instructions that are either illegal or immoral.

Constructive dismissal occurs when an employer creates conditions that make it impossible for an employee to continue working for the organization and in that way forcing them to resign. This usually happens when the employer breaches the fundamental terms of an employment contract, for example not being able to pay the salary and benefits as originally agreed. Where there is constructive dismissal the employee can take action against the employer along the same lines as those of an unfair dismissal.

Organizational justice has been associated with positive outcomes such as employee engagement, health and well-being, performance and teamwork.

7.7. TRANSPARENCY

SME governance issues relating to transparency usually focus on recruitment and promotion procedures, remuneration and grading of jobs. This is even more so in family-owned businesses where there is a mixture of family and non-family employees -remuneration and promotion practices tend to be unclear. Parts of remunerations elements have been discussed in earlier sections. In view of the need for SMEs to establish policies in the interest of transparency, this section provides some guidelines for coming up with such policies. The remuneration committee or in its absence the board must ensure that the remuneration policy is based on some defendable basis. Use of a job evaluation system provides such a basis.

7.7.1. Transparency in Recruitment

The process of recruiting skills into the organization needs to be guided by the strategic objectives and proper calculation of workforce demand. The temptation in most family businesses is to be guided by the needs of family members who need jobs with less emphasis placed on the real needs of the business. An organization's strategic plan informs what activities will be undertaken, how they will be undertaken and the resources that would be needed drive recruitment and selection. The how part of strategy implementation determine how the organization can be best designed, what organization structure would be best-fit to achieve strategic objectives and what skills and competences are required and therefore what specific jobs need to be filled. Engaging in deliberate workforce planning ensures that an organization has the right number of people, with the right competencies and attitudes, at the right place, at the right time and at the right price. It is critical for SMEs because the cost of getting it wrong can destroy a business.

In conducting workforce planning an SME needs to consider factors such as:

- Economic uncertainty;
- Hostile economic climate;
- Need to retain critical talent;
- Changes to business models,
- Changing customer demands;
- Changes in organizational culture.

Figure 7.7 summarizes the stages of the recruitment process.

Figure 7.7: Recruitment Process.

Having a formalized and documented recruitment process reduces chances of making decisions that are not based on the needs of the organization and also provides an audit trail of decisions made during the process making it more transparent. The absence of formal recruitment procedures in SMEs results in focusing on recruiting people already known to the business owners or to their managers. This compromises the organization's ability to attract the best skills. Recruitment can target either internal job applicants or the external market. SMEs usually have poor record keeping which compromises their ability to tap into skills already resident in the organization. Further, when targeting those outside the organization the targeting tends to be too focused as a way of minimizing associated costs. Having formal recruitment procedures improves the governance of the recruitment process. Guiding procedures clarify issues such as:

- Recruitment methods
- Recruitment sources

7.7.1.1. Recruitment Methods

Recruitment methods vary depending on whether the recruitment is targeting employees within the organization or outsiders. The organization's recruitment guidelines which managers would need to comply with identify the organizations preferred methods. Table 7.3 some commonly used methods.

Table 7.6: Recruitment Methods

Internal	External
- Notice board job posting - E-mail based job announcement - In-house newsletter - Company website - Employee referrals	- Media campaigns – newspapers, magazines, radio, television - Social media networks - Colleges and universities notice boards and newsletters - Company website - Internet based commercial job boards - Professional associations and organizations - Head hunters - Participation at relevant trade exhibitions - Employment agencies

7.7.1.2. Recruitment Sources

Main recruitment sources are internal and external. Internal recruitment is more cost-effective and is ideal for organization in stable environments or those in unstable environments but have financially limitations. Internal recruitment is practiced where there is a deliberate policy of promoting from within. External recruitment is ideal in situations where the environment is unstable and there is need to inject change into the organization. This may include the need to overhaul the management team. Table 7.4 presents a comparative summary of the two approaches.

Table 7.7: Pros and Cons of External and Internal Recruitment

Source	Advantages	Disadvantages
Internal recruitment	- Applicant performance data available - Motivates applicant and other employees - Faster filling of positions - Less time spent on orientation - Less costly - More chances of getting a best-fit candidate	- Subject to organizational politics - Losers may be demoralized - May create dysfunctional competition - Inbreeding problems - Unintentional creation of a tall organization
External recruitment	- Provides fresh perspectives - Increased choice - Chances for increasing the knowledge base	- Candidate are unknown entities - Discourages interested internal aspirants - Needs orientation with risk of failure - No automatic cultural fit - More expensive in terms of the process and the expected salary

7.8. TRANSPARENCY IN THE GRADING OF JOBS

Determination of the relative worth of jobs is achieved through conducting a job evaluation exercise which entails preparing job descriptions which is preceded by analyzing the jobs to get a complete understanding of the constituents, evaluating the worth of each constituent part based on given guidelines, allocating the job a grade or total points and grouping it or classifying it with similar other jobs of equal worth.

7.8.1. Job Analysis

Job analysis involves systematically analyzing the tasks and activities involved in executing a job including the level of responsibility, experience, skills, know-how and capabilities needed for the satisfactory performance of the job. The analysis also captures information relating to the physical working conditions of a job and pressure of work. The information collected during the analysis stage is used to develop the job profile or description and job evaluation focuses on those elements of the job that are captured in the job description.

7.8.2. Job Description

The requirements and responsibilities of a job are captured in the job descriptions and these constitute the basis for an organizations compensation philosophy as they ideally collectively represent the activities that need to be undertaken or "purchased" for the organization to achieve its strategic objectives and realize its mission and vision. When a reward system goes wrong and fails to reflect the organization's reason to be in terms of spending more where it matters most to the organization, the problem can be traced back to poorly structured job descriptions.

7.8.3. Job Evaluation

Job evaluation is a systematic process of determining the relative worth of jobs based on factors derived from the job analysis which are contained in the job description. Such factors include the content of the job; the basic qualifications; special training and experience required to perform it; the types of decisions it makes, for example simple, tactical, pragmatic or strategic; the resources for which it is responsible and its physical and mental demands. There are four common methods of job evaluation: ranking, classification, point-factor rating and factor comparison.

7.8.4. Ranking

Ranking involves the arrangement of jobs from highest to lowest based on for example their perceived value to the organization, their level of difficulty; and the qualifications required to perform the job. The ranking of the jobs then guide the determination of pay levels with the highest ranked job receiving the highest basic pay and the lowest ranked receiving the lowest. Methods commonly used for ranking jobs are Ordering, Weighting and Paired Comparison. Jobs are ranked by department and the departmental rankings are combined to produce an organization-wide ranking.

7.8.5. Classification

Predetermined number of job classes is established together with detailed specifications of the characteristics of each job class. Jobs are assigned to the classes based on their objective aspects without regard for the people holding the positions. Focus is on factors such as the range of job activities, level of authority and responsibilities, decisions made in the job, the magnitude of the consequences of making a wrong decision, and the level of relationships the job has to maintain. The output is a grouping of jobs into classes or grades.

7.8.6. Point-Factor Rating

Jobs are expressed in terms of their key factors which are allocated points based on order of importance. Jobs with similar points are placed in the same grade and the applicable wage is based on adding the points allocated to the factors. The critical part of the method is ensuring that factors are exhaustively defined and clearly sub-divided into sub-factors in order of importance along a clear scale that indicates the minimums, maximums and ranges. Job factors are slotted on the scale, added and the total points indicate the group the job belongs to. An amount can be allocated to each factor resulting in the monetary value of a job.

7.8.7. Factor Comparison

Factor comparison involves identifying four to five critical compensable factors for a job and then using benchmark jobs that capture the compensable factors. The benchmark jobs should be not representative in the sense of being neither overpaid nor underpaid, represent as range of the identified factors in terms of being high or low. A monetary value is attached to the job and the value is divided by the number of compensable factors to get the rate of pay for each factor.

Job evaluation enables the organization to link job worth to pay in as close to objective manner as is practically possible. Because it is based on systematic procedures that are backed by guidelines, the value attached to jobs can be checked and should the job change there is a clear basis for making adjustments to pay. Where objectively implemented it results in an equitable basic pay structure. Where there are disagreements the reasons are clearer and can be addressed in as objective a manner as is possible. The job evaluation process is participatory as employees, unions and management all are involved in coming up with the relative worth of the jobs.

Table 7.8: Illustration of a Schedule of Graded Jobs

Position	Reports to	Level	Job Factors
COO	CEO	2	Strategic decisions; Post graduate qualifications & extensive relevant experience; serious consequences of error impacting organisational performance and survival; supervised through reporting on key strategic deliverables
CFO	CEO		
CSSO	CEO		
VP Direct Distribution VP indirect Distribution VP Exclusive Sales	COO	3	Tactical decisions; university level qualification & relevant experience; serious consequences of error impacting organisational performance; supervised through timed reports tied to delivery of high level objectives
VP Strategic Planning internal Audit	CEO		
VP Sales Operations VP Financial Operations VP Financial Planning	Chief Finance Officer		
VP HR & Administration VP IT VP Supply Chain	CSSO		
Managers	All sections	4	Pragmatic decisions; relevant tertiary qualification; errors are not obvious, but through poor supervision can accumulate to substantial amounts and decay of goodwill; supervised through management by objectives
Sales Executives			
Senior Clerical Personnel			
Clerical & Admin Support	All sections	5	Simple decisions; high level of literacy and numeracy; may need to have some specific relevant skill; errors can result in wasted material and time; supervised through direct control of work done
General Support	All sections	6	Simple decisions; no required level of education; errors are obvious but have limited impact on organisational performance; supervised through direct control of work as it progresses

7.9. DEVELOPMENT OF GRADE BASED PAY STRUCTURE

A salary structure is a matrix that illustrates the levels of pay in an organization from the lowest to the highest paid position. It illustrates the minimum and maximum levels of pay for each job grade, the rate at which salaries within the same grade can vary, and the extent of differences between the pay level of one grade and that of the next grade. It is a critical tool as it provides the organization with a rough indicator of the salary budget going into the future.

The following factors are taken into consideration in developing the base pay structure:

- Perceived contribution of a job as captures through job evaluation and grading;
- Employer's perception of employees as captured in the organization's rewards philosophy, demand;
- Supply factors on the labor market; and
- Current and projected economic conditions which could affect capacity to pay.

Grouping of jobs through job evaluation provides the basis for developing pay grades which are a conglomeration of different jobs which according to the evaluation exercise have the same worth of contribution to organizational goals and therefore can be allocated the same monetary value. Pay grades usually have an applicable minimum, midpoint and maximum with ranges from minimum to maximum guided by the organization's reward philosophy. Some pay grades allow for overlaps between grades while others maintain distinct differences between grades. The number of grades on a pay structure is influenced by the organization's structure whether it is tall or flat, and by the range of jobs. When the range of jobs is wide the pay grades are likely to be either more or few but with wider pay ranges within each grade, or more overlap between grades.

The amount of pay allocated to individual employees within a pay grade is based on factors such as experience and merit. Whether an organization uses merit or experience or even both is influenced by its rewards philosophy. In organization where merit is emphasized ahead of experience and or years served in the position it is possible for newer employees to, overtime, earn higher than the long-serving employees. In organizations whose philosophy is to reward long-service it is almost impossible for late comers to end up earning more than longer serving employees doing a similar or similarly graded position. Regardless of the method used, what is critical is transparency.

7.9.1. Transparency in Employee Promotion

Another area that needs transparency and fairness is employee promotion. Promotion procedures must be clear and understood. Absence of clear procedures can expose the organization to accusations of discrimination, victimization and favoritism. Linked to promotion are policies that guide employee development for purposes of future promotion. Where as in large organizations there are many promotion opportunities within the organization and employees do not have to necessarily leave the organization in order to get bigger assignments with opportunities for growth, it is not the case in SMEs. Promotions in the latter are fewer and in some cases are perceived to be effected in a non-transparent manner. With the governance structures of an SME the board or leader has to find ways of compensating for limited promotion opportunities. Embracing Senge's (1994) characteristics of learning organizations can compensate for the dearth of promotion opportunities. In such organizations Senge posits that:

- Employees find meaning in the work they do at both a personal and global level as the continuously engage in improving their capacities.
- The combined intelligence of all organizational members is valued.
- Attempts are made to align employee personal visions to that of the organization.
- Employees are given opportunities to learn what happens at every level of the organization, have the freedom to query assumptions and biases and in that way get to understand the interrelatedness.
- There is mutual respect and trust across reporting levels.

7.10. SUMMARY AND CONCLUSION

This chapter covered fairness and transparency dimensions of corporate governance in SMEs. While fairness covers an organization's dealings with all its stakeholders, the chapter focused on fairness issues in relation to the employer–employee relationship. In that regard, it discussed executive compensation, discipline and grievance procedures, workplace democracy, employee relations and the international aspect of workplace relations as stipulated by the ILO. Forms of organizational justice were highlighted together with factors that contribute to the different forms of justice. Transparency was discussed in the context of recruitment and promotion procedures, grading of jobs through job evaluation and determination of pay scales.

QUESTIONS AND EXERCISES

1. What corporate governance issues arise in the recruitment and promotion of employees in SMEs and family businesses?

2. Discuss organizational justice and its relationship with SME corporate governance.

3. Fairness and transparency are critical factors in SME corporate governance. Discuss this statement by giving appropriate examples.

REFERENCES AND FURTHER READING

1. Bebchuk, L. A., & Fried, J. M., (2003). *Executive compensation as an agency problem* (No. w9813). National Bureau of Economic Research.

2. Bender, R., & Moir, L., (2006). Does 'best practice' in setting executive pay in the UK encourage 'good 'behavior?. *Journal of Business Ethics, 67*(1), 75–91.

3. Bizjak, J. M., Lemmon, M. L., & Naveen, L., (2008). Does the use of peer groups contribute to higher pay and less efficient compensation?. *Journal of Financial Economics, 90*(2), 152–168.

4. Bognanno, M. L., (2010). Executive compensation: A brief review. DETU Working Paper No. 10–02, Temple.

5. Chen, A., Pelger, M., & Sandmann, K., (2013). New performance-vested stock option schemes. *Applied Financial Economics, 23*(8), 709–727.

6. Dalton, D. R., Hitt, M. A., Certo, S. T., & Dalton, C. M., (2007). 1 The Fundamental Agency Problem and Its Mitigation: Independence, Equity, and the Market for Corporate Control. *The academy of Management Annals, 1*(1), 1–64.

7. Dong, Z., Wang, C., & Xie, F., (2010). Do executive stock options induce excessive risk-taking?. *Journal of Banking and Finance, 34*(10), 2518–2529.

8. Dow, J., & Raposo, C. C., (2005). CEO compensation, change, and corporate strategy. *The Journal of Finance, 60*(6), 2701–2727.

9. Ebert, F. C., Torres, R., & Papadakis, K., (2008). *Executive Compensation: Trends and Policy Issues*. IILS.

10. Efendi, J., Srivastava, A., & Swanson, E. P., (2007). Why do corporate managers misstate financial statements? The role of option compensation and other factors. *Journal of Financial Economics, 85*(3), 667–708.

11. Eisenhardt, K. M., (1989). Agency theory: An assessment and review. *Academy of management review, 14*(1), 57–74.

12. Ferri, F. & Maber, D. A., (2013). Say on pay votes and CEO compensation: Evidence from the UK. *Review of Finance, 17*(2), 527–563.

13. Fich, E. M., Tran, A. L., & Walkling, R. A., (2013). On the importance of golden parachutes. *Journal of Financial and Quantitative Analysis,*

48(06), 1717–1753.

14. Foss, N., & Stea, D., (2014). Putting a Realistic Theory of Mind into Agency Theory: Implications for Reward Design and Management in Principal-Agent Relations. *European Management Review, 11*(1), 101–116.

15. Frydman, C. & Jenter, D., (2010). *CEO compensation* (No. w16585). National Bureau of Economic Research.

16. Hall, B. J. &.Liebman, J. B., (2000). The taxation of executive compensation. In *Tax Policy and the Economy, Volume 14,* 1–44. MIT Press.

17. Harris, J., & Bromiley, P. (2007). Incentives to cheat: The influence of executive compensation and firm performance on financial misrepresentation. *Organization Science, 18*(3), 350–367.

18. Harris, J. D., (2009). What's wrong with executive compensation?. *Journal of Business Ethics, 85*(1), 147–156.

19. ILO. 2014. Rules of the Game: a brief introduction to International Labor Standards (Revised edition 2014)

20. Jensen, M. C. & Murphy, K. J., (1990). Performance pay and top-management incentives. *Journal of political economy*, 225–264.

21. Lorsch, J. W. & Khurana, R., (2010). The pay problem. *Harvard Magazine*, May–June.

22. Lowenstein, R., 2017. CEO pay is out of control: Here's how to rein it in. http://fortune.com/2017/04/19/executive-compensation-ceo-pay/

23. Lubatkin, M., Lane, P. J., Collin, S., & Very, P., (2007). An embeddedness framing of governance and opportunism: towards a cross-nationally accommodating theory of agency. *Journal of Organizational Behavior, 28*(1), 43–58.

24. Mitnick, B. M., (2013). Origin of the theory of agency: an account by one of the theory's originators. *Available at SSRN 1020378.*

25. Murphy, K. J., (1999). Executive compensation. *Handbook of labor economics, 3*, 2485–2563.

26. Murphy, K. J., (2012). Executive compensation: Where we are, and how we got there. *Handbook of the Economics of Finance. Elsevier Science North Holland (Forthcoming).*

27. Pepper, A., & Gore, J., (2015). Behavioral agency theory new

foundations for theorizing about executive compensation. *Journal of management, 41*(4), 1045–1068.

28. Pfeffer, J., (1998). *The Human Equation: Building Profits by Putting People First*. Harvard Business Press.

29. Roberts, J., (2007). *The Modern Firm: Organizational Design for Performance and Growth*. Oxford University Press.

30. Rost, K. & Weibel, A., (2013). CEO pay from a social norm perspective: The infringement and reestablishment of fairness norms. *Corporate Governance: An International Review, 21*(4), 351–372.

31. Rynes, S. L., & Gerhart, B., (2000). Compensation in organizations. *Current Research and Practice, 12 Edition in SIOP Frontiers Series*.

32. Tosi, H., Bebchuk, L., & Fried, J., (2005). Pay without performance: The unfulfilled promise of executive compensation.

33. Wade, J. B., O'Reilly III, C. A. & Pollock, T. G., (2006). Overpaid CEOs and underpaid managers: Fairness and executive compensation. *Organization Science, 17*(5), 527–544.

34. Walsh, J. P., (2008). CEO compensation and the responsibilities of the business scholar to society. *The Academy of Management Perspectives, 22*(2), 26–33.

35. Welbourne, T. M., (2004). HR Metrics for HR Strategists. *IHRIM. link.*

36. Wiseman, R. M., Cuevas-Rodríguez, G. & Gomez-Mejia, L. R., (2012). Towards a social theory of agency. *Journal of Management Studies, 49*(1), 202–222.

8
CHAPTER

CG AND CORPORATE SOCIAL RESPONSIBILITY

Chapter Aims and Objectives

By the end of this chapter, you will have a working knowledge of the relationship between corporate governance and Corporate Social Responsibility (CSR). Specifically you will:

- Be familiar with various definitions of corporate social responsibility and the pillars of CSR;
- Understand the contextual and situational nature of CSR;
- Appreciate distinguishing features of corporate social responsibility as compared to CG;
- Understand two models of CSR: Carrolls' pyramid and Dahlsrud's five dimensions model;
- Learn about perspectives on why organizations adopt corporate social responsibility practices;
- Pillars of CSR: strategic governance; human capital; stakeholder capital and environment;
- Appreciate the dark side of CSR.

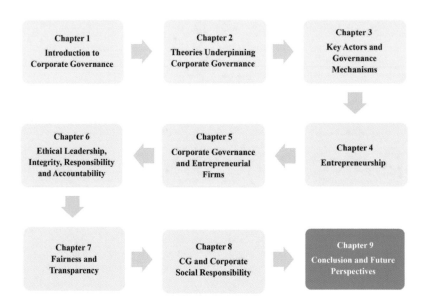

8.1. INTRODUCTION

CG focuses on the internal governance mechanism of a company as relates to safeguarding the interests of first and foremost the shareholders. Following the Enron and other related debacles there has been a growing shift in corporate governance towards going beyond the Board-management; shareholder – Board relationship to include the corporate's responsibility to other stakeholders through embracing Corporate Social Responsibility (CSR). Where corporate governance is largely grounded on agency theory, corporate social responsibility is grounded in stakeholder theory with its primary concern being that of balancing stakeholder interests as opposed to owners of capital dominating the relationship.

Global Corporate Social responsibility Policies Project (2003 cited in Dahlsrud 2008, Appendix) defined corporate social responsibility as "business practices based on ethical values and respect for workers, communities and the environment." The Green paper of the EC on corporate social responsibility (cited in Calveras, 2013) classifies corporate social responsibility policies into two dimensions: internal and external. The former encompass policies and practices relating to human resources management and environmental impact management while the latter focus on relations with external stakeholders such as the communities, customers, human rights and ecological issues. In defining internal corporate social responsibility Mory, Wirtz, and Göttel (2016) focus on Dahlrud's stakeholder dimension specifically on how organizations interact with their employees. Also focusing on internal CSR, Shen and Benson (2016) use the term 'socially responsible human resources management' to refer to corporate social responsibility directed to an organization's employees.

Studies have related employee perceptions of an organization's corporate social responsibility practices to employee commitment (Hofman and Newman, 2014), job performance and organizational citizenship (Hofman and Newman, 2014; Newman, Nielsen, and Miao, 2015), employee attitudes and job satisfaction (De Roeck et al., 2014); and engagement (Glavas, 2016). Further, firm level good labor relations have been considered as a component of corporate social responsibility (Shen and Zhu, 2011 citing Jenkins, Pearson and Seyfang, 2002).

CSR is another concept whose definition is evolving with disagreement amongst businesses, governments and NGOs in terms of where it starts and ends. To that end it has multiple definitions as illustrated in Figure 8.1.

"Social responsibility of business is to encompass the economic, legal, ethical and discretionary expectations that society has of organizations at a given point in time" (Carroll, 1979).

"CSR is the ethical behaviour of a company towards society; management acting responsibly in its relationship with other stakeholders who have a legitimate interest in the business, and it is the commitment by business to behave ethically and contribute to economic development while improving the quality of life of the workforce and their families as well as the local community and society at large" (World Business Council for Sustainable Development, 1999).

"Corporate social responsibility is essentially a concept whereby companies decide voluntarily to contribute to a better society and a cleaner environment. At a time when the European Union endeavours to identify its common values by adopting a Charter of Fundamental Rights, an increasing number of European companies recognise their social responsibility more and more clearly and consider it as part of their identity. This responsibility is expressed towards employees and more generally towards all the stakeholders affected by business and which in turn can influence its success" (Commission of the European Communities, 2001).

"CSR is a commitment to improve community well-being through discretionary business practices and contributions of corporate resources" (Kotler & Lee, 2005).

"CSR is the commitment of business to contribute to sustainable economic development-working with employees, their families, the local community and society at large to improve the quality of life in ways that are both good for business and good for development" (World Bank, 2008).

Figure 8.1. Corporate social responsibility Definitions.

With globalization and increased reporting there is pressure on companies and directors to take into account not only the owners of the business in company operations but to also consider other stakeholders such as the employees, the community, suppliers, customers and the environment.

Acting in a manner that gives due consideration to all stakeholders is acting in a responsible manner and is corporate social responsibility. Corporate social responsibility goes against Friedman's (1962) view that the only responsibility of business is to generate profits for the shareholder. Corporate social responsibility in that regard is viewed as an unnecessary additional cost. However, globalization, activism etc. have placed it within corporate governance as one of key issues of operating a business. Corporate Social Responsibility (CSR) is about companies acting as good corporate social citizens. The rationale behind corporate social responsibility is that since corporate entities are sanctioned and promoted by society and since society legitimates business by allowing them to function and to use the scarce resources while providing them with an environment that allows them to earn profits it is fair for society to expect businesses to be good corporate citizens that obey society's laws and refrain from activities that have negative social and environmental impacts. To that effect, the scope of corporate entities must extend beyond mere profit making to playing a proactive role in finding solutions to society's many problems and to engage in activities aimed at improving society's welfare, even doing so reduces economic profits.

The success of business entity is partly dependent on its image with a positive image associated with increase in profitability in the long run. A good image establishes confidence, loyalty, trust, and stronger relations with stakeholders. To that effect engaging in corporate social responsibility goes beyond altruism.

8.2. MODELS OF CSR

Carroll (1979) proposes that corporate social responsibility has is made up of four kinds of social responsibilities: economic, legal, ethical and philanthropic. The economic and legal components of Carroll's responsibilities are also covered by corporate governance as they relate to profit making and compliance. The other two are what perhaps differentiates corporate social responsibility from CG.

8.2.1. Ethical Component

Corporates are expected to conduct their business in a manner consistent with the ethical norms of the environment in which they are operating. Corporate integrity means more than just complying with laws and regulations.

8.2.2. Philanthropic component

Corporates are expected to meet charitable expectations of societies in which they operate by for example being seen to alleviate poverty, participation in charitable and life enhancing activities.

According to Carroll the four kinds of social responsibilities exist on a pyramid: at the bottom of the pyramid and serving as the base of the structure is economic performance followed by legal because of the need for the business to operate within the stipulated legal framework; next is ethics that speak to the need for a business to behave in a fair, just and right manner and finally is philanthropy which involves a business contributing time and resources for the betterment of the community.

Dahlsrud (2008) presents corporate social responsibility as five dimensional the dimensions being: environmental; social; economic; stakeholder and voluntariness.

- Environmental refers to conducting business in an environmentally responsible manner in terms of a cleaner environment, preservation of flora and fauna.

- Social refers to the impact the business makes in the communities in which it is operating. This may include minimization or elimination of activities with long-term negative impact and improvement of livelihoods.

- Economic dimension refers to the business operating profitably and as a result improving standards of living, paying fair wages, and distributing generated wealth equitably.

- Stakeholder interaction refers to the maintenance of mutual respect, respect of rights and values of all those impacted on by the operations of the business.

- Voluntariness refers to the business participating in activities that go beyond what is a legal requirement or is mandated by professional or industry regulations. Voluntariness is purely driven by the company's conscience in the face of situation where assistance is needed.

Dahlsrud's (2008) voluntariness, stakeholder interactions and social have close resemblance to Carroll's ethical and philanthropic as they are not driven by regulation and compliance. Environmental and Economic dimensions have a close relationship to corporate governance practices. Environmental is usually driven from clearly spelt out frameworks that may or may not be linked to some legislation while the economic dimension is linked to the need to enhance shareholder returns.

Looking at both Dahlsrud and Carrolls' views of what constitutes CSR, it is clear that there is an element of overlap between corporate social responsibility and corporate governance. Like corporate governance in implementing CSR, one size does not fit all. In large companies there are standardized procedures of handling CSR. In some cases these are embedded in organizational strategies and are guided by policies formulated at Board level. For SMEs and family businesses these are more likely to be ad hoc.

Corporate social responsibility and corporate governance are central to managing the relationship between business and society as they can add value to companies whilst maintaining a good relationship with society (Harjoto and Jo, 2011). Corporate governance on its own cannot address all the needs relating to the relationship between business and its various stakeholders, it, however, provides mechanisms for business involvement in corporate social responsibility activities, reporting on them and incorporating them within business plans.

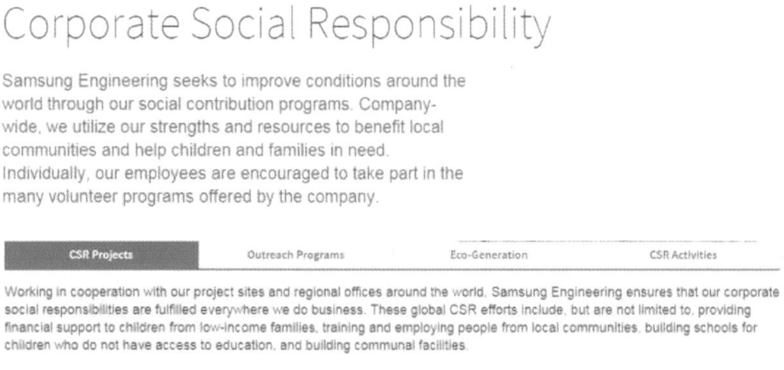

Figure 8.2: Samsung Engineering corporate social responsibility Reporting, Source: http://www.samsungengineering.com/sustainability/corporate/project/suView.

8.3. WHY ORGANIZATIONS ENGAGE IN CORPORATE SOCIAL RESPONSIBILITY

The rationale for organizations' participation in corporate social responsibility activities can be viewed from three perspectives: the values level argument, the risk mitigation argument, the public relations argument and the dark side of corporate social responsibility.

8.3.1. Values Level Argument

Ethical considerations are more about values than about rules. An organization engages in corporate social responsibility voluntarily and not for purposes of fulfilling rules. It is a way of a company expressing who it is as a corporate citizen and what it considers important in its relationship with society and the environment. Increasingly corporate governance is incorporating values which moves it from being a purely compliance and agent-principal relations management tool to a focus on how the corporate is seen by outsiders – a process that goes more into actual visible actions that are in the public domain than ticking of boxes in the board rooms. Claims to good corporate governance have not always been aligned with good corporate citizenship or with ethical behavior. The Enron debacle occurred in an organization that laid claim to practicing good corporate governance. Governance that is based on values is driven by altruistic motives and goes beyond technical box ticking to include concerns about the social and environmental impact of the company's products and or services in both the short and long-term. However, to address these, corporate social responsibility issues need to be mainstreamed into a company's corporate governance structures.

8.3.2. Risk Level Convergence

According to the risk level convergence view, corporate social responsibility and corporate governance interface at the point of managing or mitigating operational risk. corporate social responsibility is engaged in for purposes of adhering to social and environmental reporting standards in line with the Global Reporting Initiative and in so doing reduce social and environmental risks. This view of corporate social responsibility is financially rather than altruistically driven. The focus is on risk mitigation as corporate social responsibility is viewed as a risk that needs to be managed. A company engages in corporate social responsibility activities to wade off pressure from non-governmental organizations and other pressure groups that could easily present risks for the business in the long-term.

According to risk level convergence view of corporate social responsibility, it is part of a board's fiduciary duty to attend to social responsibility risks facing the business as good corporate citizenship is good for business. For example, companies have to ensure fair treatment in their relationships with both suppliers and customers as both can expose the company to negative perceptions. Reporting on for example sustainable procurement strategies and policies can enhance a company's reputational capital. The clothing industry has a reputation for using child labor. Samsung attracted negative publicity over shortcomings in its supply chain (Figure 8.3). This makes it imperative for companies in that sector to have strong corporate social responsibility programs that illustrate their role in alleviating this problem and also in assuring society that their suppliers are not involved in any human rights abuses.

> # Samsung finds labour violations at dozens of its Chinese suppliers
>
> Annual report says there are breaches of working time, safety equipment provision and discipline, but no child labour
>
> Samsung says that an external audit found labour violations at dozens of its suppliers in China, including failure to provide safety gear and excessive working hours, but that none involved child workers.
>
> The findings covered 100 of its Chinese suppliers - which number over 200 - and were outlined in its annual corporate social responsibility report.
>
> "A majority of suppliers do not comply with China's legally permitted overtime hours," says page 69 of the report (PDF), saying that it demanded those suppliers reduce overtime.
>
> Samsung has already come under fire in its home country of south Korea over its response to claims that chemicals in one of its chip factories caused leukaemia and led to the deaths of a number of workers.
>
> The company has apologised for the length of time it took to provide compensation, while saying that it does not accept there was a link.
>
> The world's largest maker of mobile phones and smartphones, Samsung has been subjected to increasing examination of its practices. In 2012 it faced allegations that its plants in China used child labourers. New York-based pressure group China Labor Watch claimed that working conditions at Samsung suppliers were "inhumane", and the company vowed to eliminate illegal overtime by the end of 2014.

Figure 8.3: Negative publicity from shortcomings in supply chain, Source: https://www.theguardian.com/technology/2014/jul/01/samsung-working-prac-tice-breaches-chinese-suppliers.

8.3.2.1. Corporate Social Responsibility as a Public Relations Exercise – Ulterior Motives

Under this perspective corporate social responsibility serves as a window dressing exercise to appease the various stakeholders – particularly publics outside the company.

8.4. FACTORS THAT SPUR CORPORATE SOCIAL RESPONSIBILITY

Factors that spur corporate social responsibility are not very different from those spurring corporate governance a situation that demonstrates the link between the two. Investors are as concerned with corporate governance issues as they are with corporate social responsibility issues. Environmental and social risks embedded in a portfolio are increasingly becoming matters of concern for investors and governments. The U.N. Environment Program's Principles for Responsible Investment (PRI) require investors to build-in environmental, social and governance issues to their investment practices. Reporting on corporate social responsibility is voluntary even for public entities. For SMEs and family businesses the bulk of which are not public entities both corporate social responsibility and corporate governance reporting are voluntary – with some exceptions. However, globalization pressures are forcing companies to report on the corporate social responsibility activities. That need to report is forcing companies to engage in and report on corporate social responsibility. Over time both the quality and quantity of reporting on corporate social responsibility has been improving and there has been a proliferation of reporting standards indicative of its importance to businesses.

8.4.1. Pillars of CSR

Where the pillars of corporate governance have been identified as accountability, assurance of independence, fairness and transparency, various have been identified for CSR as indicated below:

- Strategic governance, human capital, stakeholder capital and the environment (Gupta, 2016).
- Ethics, leadership, personal responsibility and trust (Isaac Mostovicz, Kakabadse and Kakabadse, 2011)
- Community, environment, workplace and market place (http://www.csrhub.ie/Ireland-s-National-Plan-on-CSR/The-Pillars/).
- Economic development, governance, environment and society (Dragon Capital).
- Leadership, values and ethics; employees and the workplace; clients; communities; suppliers and business partners; and the environment (Capgemini, 2010).

Although the pillars have some similarities they are also different. Just like in the case of corporate governance what constitutes CSR varies from organization to organization. What is critical is the existence of a commonly understood position on what constitutes corporate social responsibility in the context of an organization.

8.5. CORPORATE SOCIAL RESPONSIBILITY GONE WRONG

Corporate social responsibility depends on businesses regulating themselves ensuring that they act is a responsible manner as already explained. Like corporate governance that looks good only on paper, the same applies to corporate social responsibility as indicated by multiple examples of failed corporate social responsibility.

8.5.1. Examples of Failed Corporate Social Responsibility

Volkswagen failed in both corporate social responsibility and corporate governance by deliberately circumventing emissions controls in order to give the company an advantage over its competitors. The question is: where was corporate governance when this was happening?

Figure 8.4: Volkswagen scandal, *Source*: http://www.bbc.com/news/business-34324772.

CSR has also been used to engage in activities not necessarily in the long-term interests of the company. Managers have been known to focus on those activities where they themselves have interests. Even in situations where corporate social responsibility decisions are handled at board level within the framework of corporate governance this has been found not to curtail conflict of interest in the administration of corporate social responsibility programs. Samsung is a case in point where an owner has been convicted of hiding behind corporate social responsibility to make donations to charities where the motive was not in the interest of the business.

8.5.2. Should It Be Voluntary or Mandatory?

One recurring question on corporate social responsibility is whether it should be mandatory or voluntary. NGOs focusing on social responsibility who would want to see more enforceable tools to force businesses to comply advocates for mandatory, regulated situations. An opposing school of thought largely held by the corporates advocates for voluntarism and self-regulation. Regardless of differing schools of thought, corporate social responsibility has become part of businesses' strategy as they seek to fulfill their interests in a more transparent manner with due consideration for social and environmental issues – a triple bottom line approach to performance. For entrepreneurial firms as defined here, both corporate governance and corporate social responsibility though not mandatory are critical for business growth in their immediate environment and at a global level.

8.6. CONVERGENCE OF CORPORATE GOVERN-ANCE AND CSR

Can we then say corporate governance and corporate social responsibility practices converge? Is there a relationship between corporate governance and CSR? Does a high-level of corporate governance translate to a high-level of CSR? Corporate governance practices that have been linked with corporate social responsibility include:
- Disclosure of social, environmental, and ethical issues;
- Accountability and transparency;
- Board composition and diversity to an extent in some cases of having a board that reflects the demographics of a business' area of operation;
- Risk management especially relating to social and cultural norms;

- Compensation of workers including other working conditions;
- Independence and expertize of directors;
- Board-level oversight of environmental and social risks;
- Linkage of executive pay and attainment of both financial and non-financial results in a manner that ensures equitable distribution of the wealth created by the business.

In the global landscape corporate governance and corporate social responsibility are becoming difficult to distinguish as they overlap and one serves as a mirror of the other. They are both linked and related. Where there is strong corporate governance there also tends to be a high-level of CSR. An organization with strong corporate governance mechanisms and with high-levels of compliance is likely to be a good corporate citizen and this is likely to be reflected in their corporate social responsibility activities. Although the two focus on different aspects of organizational governance, they cannot be separated. While the economic component of corporate governance relating to maximisation of shareholder value and legal compliance and investment risk management are better handled under board mechanisms, the components that relate to ethics such as social and environmental issues are better handled under CSR. Generally corporate social responsibility initiatives need funding and in that regard depend on the economic side of corporate governance. Because entrepreneurial organizations, especially SMEs tend to have financial challenges, they tend to be weaker in both corporate governance and CSR.

The strong linkages have led to come recommending that corporate social responsibility which includes issues of sustainability should be incorporated within corporate governance and that there must be mandatory reporting in order to ensure transparency (Sharma and Khanna, 2014). In large companies corporate social responsibility reporting is incorporated into their corporate governance structures. This results in enhancement of investor accountability to other stakeholders. The reports are usually in the form of corporate social responsibility board committees; policy pronouncements and ethics codes of conduct. The reports cover varied areas such as employees, environmental and societal matters.

Reporting on employee issues covers employee engagement and satisfaction, pay and benefits, respect for employee rights; training and development, workplace diversity, safety, health and well being, and long-service recognition and appreciation. Reporting on environmental issues includes energy conservation, reduction of carbon dioxide emissions, contributions towards building a sustainable future and occupational health and safety. It is part of what is generally termed "sustainability reporting." Guidelines for sustainability reporting are provided by, for example, the Global Reporting Initiative (GRI). The GRI assists organizations to appreciate the effect their operations have on environmental issues such as climate change, environmental degradation, human rights and corruption. Although sustainability reporting is generally associated with big organizations, the increasing focus on environmental issues is making it imperative for SMEs to incorporate environmental issues in their corporate governance structures. GRI has provided guidelines specifically for SME sustainability reporting. The following benefits have been associated with SME sustainability reporting:

- Strengthening of internal systems through incorporating sustainability issues into the strategic plan, tracking company data for purposes of reporting also benefits other internal processes, builds in capacity to identify errors and other potential risks early and motivates employees.

- Externally relationships with other stakeholders are strengthened, the reputation of the company is enhanced making it attractive to investors and customers.

8.6.1. Global Focus on Sustainable Development

There is growing global focus on sustainable development as illustrated by the United Nations' sustainable development goals (SDGs). This has implications for corporate governance in SMEs as SDGs focus on areas pertinent to SME operations which are:

- Environmental issues incorporating climate change, waste and pollution and water scarcity;

- Social issues incorporating food security and urbanization;

- Human rights and equality;

Given the role played by SMEs in most national economies, they need to align their strategic plans to address the SDGs both for purposes of complying and making their businesses attractive to external parties who include consumers of their products and services and investment partners. Some specific governance issues SMEs can address in this regard are:

- Employee friendly working conditions where there are no forms of discrimination;

- Positive human relations in the company where all employee rights are respected;
- Contribution towards alleviating poverty in the immediate community;
- Adopting responsible business practices that ensure continuous improvement and sustainability.
- Adopting transparent sustainability reporting where there is openness about the company's values, governance model, and perhaps most important, the impact of its operations on other stakeholders.
- Clearly report on the company's stakeholders and their respective interests in the businesses and how the company is addressing the interests.
- Indicating action taken to address identified shareholder concerns and any industry applicable standards, policies and regulations.

8.7. SUMMARY AND CONCLUSION

This chapter discussed the relationship between corporate governance and CSR. It started by introducing corporate social responsibility through looking at its various definitions and noting that like corporate governance it has multiple definitions and to that extent its application may be both contextual and situational. A distinguishing feature of corporate social responsibility as compared to corporate governance was highlighted as that of focus. While corporate governance focuses on economic factors and legal compliance, corporate social responsibility was noted to be more on the side of ethics focusing on social and environmental issues. Corporate social responsibility was noted to have two dimensions – internal relating to employees and relationships within the business and external relating to the rest of society and environmental issues. The chapter proceeded to discuss models of corporate social responsibility specifically Carrolls' pyramid model and Dahlsrud's five dimensions model. Perspectives on why organizations adopt corporate social responsibility practices were highlighted as the values level argument, the risk mitigation argument, the public relations argument. It was noted that in all this there is a dark side of corporate social responsibility where it is used to buy favors. Some cases of where corporate social responsibility has gone wrong were presented. Finally the chapter discussed the convergence of corporate social responsibility and corporate governance. The criticality of SMEs reporting on sustainability issues in line with global trends was highlighted.

The next chapter looks at the future of corporate social responsibility.

QUESTIONS AND EXERCISES

"All this does not mean, however, that Samsung always has the respect of the people. Repeated tax-dodging scandals and suspicions of bribery have made the company a regular target of anti-corporate sentiment. For more than a year, former employees and their family members have been staging sit-in rallies in front of Samsung's office in Gangnam demanding an apology and compensation for workers at its semiconductor factory who have been diagnosed with leukemia. Perhaps the final straw came on Friday morning when the Seoul Central District Court approved the arrest warrant for Lee, which special prosecutors had sought. The 48-year-old heir is suspected of paying 43bn won ($37.3m) to two foundations controlled by Choi Soon-sil, a longtime friend of President Park Geun-hye, in return for political favors" (Samsung arrest imperils company and country. https://www.ft.com/content/da80812a-f52f-11e6-8758-6876151821a6).

1. Discuss the above Samsung case in the context of corporate governance and corporate social responsibility.

2. Using an organization you are familiar with illustrate how it could benefit from adopting sustainability reporting based on some internationally recognized guidelines.

REFERENCES AND FURTHER READING

1. Alonso-Almeida, M., Llach, J., & Marimon, F., (2014). A closer look at the 'Global Reporting Initiative' sustainability reporting as a tool to implement environmental and social policies: A worldwide sector analysis. *Corporate Social Responsibility and Environmental Management, 21*(6), 318–335.

2. Bolton, S. C., Kim, R. C. & O'Gorman, K. D., (2011). Corporate social responsibility as a dynamic internal organizational process: A case study, *Journal of Business Ethics 101*(1), 61–74

3. Cadbury Report, (1992). *Report of the Committee on the Financial Aspects of Corporate Governance*, London: Burgess Science Press.

4. CapGemini, (2010). *Corporate Social Responsibility and Sustainability*. Retrieved from https://www.capgemini.com/be-en/wp-content/uploads/sites/17/2017/12/crs_framework_brochure_rework-new.pdf

5. Carroll, A., (1979). 'A three dimensional conceptual model of corporate performance', *Academy of Management Review, 4*(4), 497–505.

6. Carroll, A. B., (1999). Corporate Social Responsibility: Evolution of a Definitional Construct. *Business and Society, 38*(3), 268–295.

7. Commission of the European Communities (2001). 'Promoting a European framework for Corporate Social Responsibility', EU Commission Green Paper COM, p. 366.

8. Dahlsrud, A., (2008). How corporate social responsibility is defined: an analysis of 37 definitions. *Corporate Social Responsibility and Environmental Management, 15*(1), 1–13.

9. Davis, K., (1960). Can business afford to ignore social responsibilities? *California Management Review, 2*(3), 497–505.

10. Dragon Capital, (n.d.). C.S.R. Pillars. *www.dragoncapital.com/.../Our-complete-Corporate-Social-Responsibility-CSR*. Retrieved from http://www.dragoncapital.com/wp-content/uploads/2016/10/Our-complete-Corporate-Social-Responsibility-CSR-Practices.pdf

11. Drucker, P. F., (2007). *People and Performance: The Best of Peter Drucker on Management*. Boston, MA: Harvard Business School Press.

12. Gill, A., (2008). Corporate governance as social responsibility: A research agenda. *Berkeley J. Int'l L., 26*, 452.

13. Global Reporting Initiative, (2014). Ready to report? Introducing

sustainability reporting for SMEs.

14. Global Reporting Initiative, (n.d.). Small business big impact SME sustainability reporting from vision to action.

15. Gupta, R., (2016). Corporate Social Responsibility and financial Performance of Indian firms. Doctoral thesis.

16. Hotten, R., (2015). Volkswagen: The Scandal explained. http://www.bbc.com/news/business-34324772

17. Isaac Mostovicz, E., Kakabadse, A. & Kakabadse, N. K., (2011). The four pillars of corporate responsibility: ethics, leadership, personal responsibility and trust. *Corporate Governance: The international journal of business in society, 11*(4), 489–500.

18. Jenkins, H., (2004). A critique of conventional corporate social responsibility theory: An SME perspective. *Journal of General Management, 29*, 37–57.

19. Kotler, P. & Lee, N., (2005). *Corporate Social Responsibility: Doing the Most Good for Your Company and Your Cause*, New Jersey: John Wiley and Sons, Inc.

20. OECD, (2004). OECD Principles of Corporate Governance, Paris: OECD.

21. Schaper, M. T. & Savery, L. K, (2004). Entrepreneurship and philanthropy: the case of small Australian firms. *Journal of Developmental Entrepreneurship, 9*(3), 239–250.

22. Sethi, S. P., (2003). Setting global standards: guidelines for creating codes of conduct in multinational corporations, Wiley, Hoboken (New Jersey).

23. Sharma, J. P., & Khanna, S., 2014. Corporate social responsibility, corporate governance and sustainability: Synergies and inter-relationships. *Indian Journal of Corporate Governance, 7*(1), 14–38.

24. Smith, R. E., (2011). Defining corporate social responsibility: A systems approach for socially responsible capitalism. University of Pennsylvania MPhil Thesis. Retrieved from https://repository.upenn.edu/od_theses_mp/9/

25. World Business Council for Sustainable Development, (1999). *Corporate Social Responsibility: Meeting Changing Expectations*, Geneva: World Business Council for Sustainable Development.

26. Zadek, S., (2004). The path to corporate social responsibility, *Harvard Business Review, 82*(12), 125–132.

9
CHAPTER

CONCLUSION AND FUTURE PERSPECTIVES

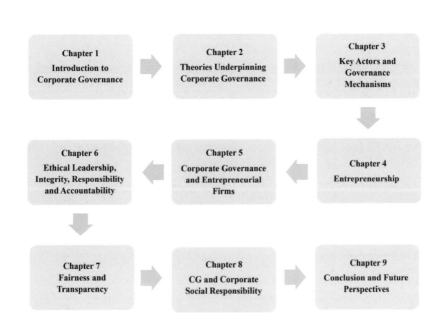

This book set out to explore corporate governance mechanisms and practices in entrepreneurial companies. It started by introducing corporate governance through its various definitions and applications largely in public companies. Key elements of corporate governance were identified together with international organizations' principles of corporate governance. The evolution of corporate governance together was explored in the context of its history. Key CSR stakeholders were identified together with their interests and the challenges encountered by companies in adopting corporate governance were discussed.

Corporate governance was noted to refer to those rules and or guidelines that are used to manage the relationship between owners of capital, management and other stakeholders. It was highlighted that corporate governance has as its basic values: transparency; accountability; responsibility; and fair treatment although in its operationalization organizations adopt those practices that are relevant to their circumstances. Organizational factors such as ownership structures, nation or region-specific environments and type of industry account for the differences. The form of corporate governance mechanisms used in any situation is derived from underlying theories the main ones being agency, stakeholder, transaction, resource dependence, social contract and political theory.

Key corporate governance actors were identified as the shareholders, the board, management and other stakeholders while corporate governance mechanisms identified were those internal and external to the firm. Internal mechanisms included the Board of Directors, management, independent internal audit, firm strategy and structure and internal reporting while external controls were identified the legal and regulatory frameworks, pressure from vocal non-governmental organizations; the managerial labor market in terms of ability to easily change organizations, and mandatory public disclosure requirements.

As part of linking corporate governance to entrepreneurial companies a chapter was dedicated to entrepreneurial firms and their characteristics in order to identify those elements that separate them from other forms of business and the implications this has for corporate governance mechanisms and practices. In looking at these firms focus was one SMEs and family businesses. It was emphasized that SMEs are not necessarily all family businesses neither are family businesses always small or medium-sized. Further, being entrepreneurial is not necessarily synonymous with being an SME or being a family-owned business.

Barriers and challenges faced by entrepreneurial businesses were discussed including the relationship between the stage of an entrepreneurial firm and its corporate governance mechanisms. The general nature of corporate governance in entrepreneurial companies and the benefits of their embracing corporate governance and the associated challenges were discussed. Business founders and owners both as individual and as families were noted to dominate corporate governance mechanisms in entrepreneurial firms. This is in sharp contrast to the situation observed for public companies.

Although corporate governance in SMEs may not necessarily focus on the role of the board, mechanisms that ensure good governance remain necessary. Two chapters were dedicated to these aspects being: ethics and integrity, responsibility, accountability, fairness and transparency.

Corporate governance practices were found to make a business a law abiding and regulations compliant corporate citizen. A chapter was dedicated to the relationship between corporate governance and CSR. The two concepts were noted to differ on focus: corporate governance focusing on economic factors and legal compliance and corporate social responsibility focusing on ethics, social and environmental issues. It was noted that clearly articulating an organization's position of corporate governance and having mechanisms in place does not necessarily translate to practice. Examples were given of cases where corporate social responsibility has gone wrong despite the existence of corporate governance mechanisms suggesting that both corporate governance and corporate social responsibility are in an evolutionary state.

The convergence of corporate social responsibility and corporate governance was discussed and it was noted that going into the future the two may converge. Research shows specific areas of balancing corporate governance and entrepreneurship. The following corporate governance challenges for entrepreneurial companies are likely to continue into the future:

- Accessing people with the right skills and experience and specific areas of expertize that are in short supply;
- Some board roles may become increasingly problematic for the board to fulfill, for example: safeguarding values and mission; shaping strategy in turbulent environments; and compliance with external (government) demands and demands of pressure groups such as strong NGOs
- Managing the tension between social and business goals

- Balancing allowing management room to run the business with the need to maintain control;

- Managing the demands of different stakeholders and regulators more so when operating at a global level – managing issues of profit with a conscience will continue to become more complex as advances in technology make information more easily accessible to many stakeholders.

Moves towards corporate accountability integrating corporate governance and corporate social responsibility issues are likely to increase. Organizations will have more say and be accountable for what their business partners such as suppliers do. Issues of environmental sustainability and respect for human rights will become issues of increasing concern for SME boards because of the associated risks. For example, there is increasing pressure for complete disclosure and transparency and traceability of goods SMEs carry in their outlets in view of global problems relating to:

- Use of child labor and or forced labor;
- Working conditions;
- Wages and inequality.

Corporate governance in entrepreneurial firms will continue to be focused more on all stakeholders and development of robust systems and procedures and less on the need to address agency problems as these tend not to exist in the same form as in public companies. With improvements in information and communication technology, everything a company does is in the public domain. It is therefore beyond complying with what is documented as acceptable but rather acting in a manner acceptable and perceived as indicative of being a responsible citizen by all stakeholders. This has implications for the way entrepreneurial companies will configure their corporate governance mechanisms. Stakeholder representation in such firms will be critical as a way of managing risks relating to failing to be seen to be addressing stakeholder expectations.

Advances in communications technology, the rise of virtual organizations, and the increasingly important role-played by SMEs in different economies corporate governance standards ordinarily associated with big organizations. SMEs will need to tighten their governance mechanism through developing clear policies and procedures that serve as a guideline for business operations. It will be critical for SMEs to learn what they can from bigger organization but to nevertheless develop governance structures that have the flexibility to adapt to the changing needs of the business.

SMEs are generally viewed as inward looking and not doing much to extend business benefits to other stakeholders. Communities are becoming more demanding from businesses operating in their environments. The demands range from demanding that they act in a socially responsible manner by addressing some of the problems faced by communities to ensuring that business in conducted in a manner that does not disrupt the environment and is therefore sustainable.

QUESTIONS AND EXERCISES

1. How do you see corporate governance in SMEs evolving?
2. What form of corporate governance mechanisms will be ideal for entrepreneurial firms?

REFERENCES AND FURTHER READING

1. Aras, G. & Crowther, D. (2016). *A Handbook of Corporate Governance and Social Responsibility*. CRC Press.

2. Aguilera, R. V., Desender, K., Bednar, M. K., & Lee, J. H., (2015). Connecting the dots: Bringing external corporate governance into the corporate governance puzzle. *Academy of Management Annals, 9*(1), 483–573.

3. Boivie, S., Bednar, M. K., Aguilera, R. V., & Andrus, J. L., (2016). Are boards designed to fail? The implausibility of effective board monitoring. *The Academy of Management Annals, 10*(1), 319–407.

4. Calabrò, A. & Mussolino, D., (2013). How do boards of directors contribute to family SME export intensity? The role of formal and informal governance mechanisms. *Journal of Management & Governance, 17*(2), 363–403.

5. Desender, K. A., Aguilera, R. V., Lópezpuertas-Lamy, M. & Crespi, R., (2016). A clash of governance logics: Foreign ownership and board monitoring. *Strategic Management Journal, 37*(2), 349–369.

6. Gnan, L., Montemerlo, D., & Huse, M., (2015). Governance systems in family SMEs: The substitution effects between family councils and corporate governance mechanisms. *Journal of Small Business Management, 53*(2), 355–381.

7. Goranova, M. & Ryan, L. V., (2014). Shareholder activism: A multidisciplinary review. *Journal of Management, 40*(5), 1230–1268.

8. Hilb, M., (2012). *New Corporate Governance: Successful Board Management Tools*. Springer Science & Business Media.

9. McCahery, J. A., Vermeulen, E. P., & Hisatake, M., (2013). The present and future of corporate governance: Re-examining the role of the board of directors and investor relations in listed companies. *European Company and Financial Law Review, 10*(2), 117–163.

10. Walls, J. L., Berrone, P., & Phan, P. H., (2012). Corporate governance and environmental performance: Is there really a link?. *Strategic Management Journal, 33*(8), 885–913.

APPENDIX

APPENDIX 1

Corporate Governance Toolkits for SMES

Given that needs of companies differ etc. – SMEs and entrepreneurs usually interested more in practice and or action – what works is a ready to use tool kit. Several have been provided. Focus here is on amalgamating them for easier usability and based on characteristics of an SME. The guide should always be that which works in the interest of the business.

Elements of an effective framework for SMEs

1. Foundational pillars
2. Structure, Composition and Membership of the Board
3. Conduct in the Boardroom – relationships and performance
4. Board committee structure
5. Disclosure and communication with shareholders
6. Risk management and compliance
7. Strategy formulation, planning and monitoring
8. Board relationship with management

9.   Corporate social responsibility

1. Foundational pillars

·   Accountability
·   Transparency
·   Controls
·   Assurance

2. Structure, Composition and Membership of the Board

Indicate whether the practices described below are there (**Yes**) or not there (**No**) in your company			
Board charter		Directors' Code of Conduct	
Director selection and appointment process		Separation of Chairman and CEO	
NED independence and objectivity		Skills/selection criteria and term of Chairman	
Remuneration		Skills/selection criteria and terms of directors	
Formal letters of appointment to directors		Appropriate size	

3. Conduct in the Boardroom – relationships and performance

Indicate whether the practices described below are there (**Yes**) or not there (**No**) in your company			
Agreed and understood roles and responsibilities		Performance evaluation	
Composition and organization		Board agenda, reporting, papers and minutes	
Induction and training		Frequency, conduct, management and outcomes of meetings	
Access to and relationship with independent advisors		Confidentiality of discussions	
Management/board relationship		Competent company secretary	

4. Board committee structure

Indicate whether the practices described below are there (**Yes**) or not there (**No**) in your company			
Charter and clarity in roles and responsibilities		Induction and training	
Structure		Relationships with third parties/access to external advice	
Skills/selection criteria and terms of chairman and members		Annual performance review	
Independence and objectivity		Relationships with third parties/access to external advice	
Frequency of meetings		Annual performance review	
Relationship with and reporting to the board			

5. Disclosure and communication with shareholders

Indicate whether the practices described below are there (**Yes**) or not there (**No**) in your company			
Communication with shareholders and stakeholders		Conflicts of interest	
Annual report disclosures		Policies and procedures	
Clear operational instructions and guidance		Definitions of role and responsibilities	
Delegations of authority		Clearly defined and well-managed relationships with stakeholders and regulators	
Disclosure of conflict of interest		Continuous disclosure obligations and company announcements	

6. Risk management and compliance

Indicate **Yes** where you agree and **No** where you do not agree that provisions are in place to address the following:			
Policy/framework		Statutory and regulatory compliance frameworks	

Board commitment, oversight and review		Communication and training	
Accountability		Monitoring, reporting and certifications	
Risk processes:		CEO/CFO statements:	
Risk identification		Financial reports present true and fair view	
Risk assessment /measurement		Effective and efficient risk management and control	
Risk response		External audit	
Robust internal controls		Internal audit	

7. Strategy formulation, planning and monitoring

Indicate whether the practices described below are there (**Yes**) or not there (**No**) in your company			
Vision and mission		Monitoring and evaluation	
Strategic/corporate plan		Management performance monitoring and assessment	
Business plans		Management succession planning	
Annual budgets		Component strategies, e.g., technology, CAPEX	

8. Board relationship with management

Indicate whether the board – management relationship described below is a true (**Yes**) or not true (**No**) description of what prevails in your company			
Clarity of roles and responsibilities		Accessible	
Value-adding		Accountable	
Open and honest		Appropriate performance-based remuneration	
Consultative		Objective performance measures	

9. Corporate Social Responsibility Checklist

Indicate **Yes** where you agree and **No** where you do not agree that provisions are in place to address the following:			
Code of Conduct/Code of Ethics		Political contributions	
Commitment to shareholders		Integrity of advertising	
Ethical standards		Employee relations	
Addressing employees expectations		Health and safety	
Privacy		Social and environmental obligations	
Compliance		Trading policy	
Conflict of interest		Whistle blowing	
Improper payments/ receipts			

INDEX

T

Transformational leadership 106, 133

Transparency 57

U

Unethical behavior 65, 69
Unethical leadership 106
Utilitarianism 105, 150

V

Vertical Chart 120

W

Walmart 96, 97, 98, 101
Weak marketing 69
Working conditions; 218
Workplace democracy 154, 175, 176, 178, 193
World Wide Fund for Nature (WWF) 46